Wicked MOBILE

BRENDAN KIRBY

THE
History
PRESS

Published by The History Press
Charleston, SC
www.historypress.net

First published 2015

Manufactured in the United States

ISBN 978.1.62619.913.2

Library of Congress Control Number: 2015948817

For Kerry, my love and my partner

CONTENTS

PREFACE

I'm not a historian, and I don't even play one on TV.

What you are about to read would not qualify as scholarly, academic research, although I put more hours of legwork than I'd like to count into it.

What I am is a storyteller. As a journalist, I have told stories for more than twenty years. Newsrooms trade in the bizarre and the macabre. Invariably, when reporters and editors share the details of some salacious story they are working on, someone will say, "You can't make this up" because the raw truth of a strange story often is more intriguing than fiction.

With all of those years writing "the first rough draft of history," as the old saying about newspapers goes, I figured I was well suited to try my hand at actual history. And this is not the dry stuff of names and dates from a history textbook. This is the stuff of "you can't make this up" scandal that I've covered in real time as a journalist. Some of this stuff, in fact, literally did end up on the front pages of newspapers.

The only difference is that it all took place long before I was born.

This is the story of the rogues and rapscallions, the corrupt politicians and vicious murderers, the unspeakable events and unthinkable people who have crawled through history over Mobile, Alabama's three centuries. I have tried to present the events in as much of a narrative form as possible while remaining faithful to the actual events.

Dialogue comes either from contemporaneous writings or historical accounts that use direct quotes. During high-profile trials in the early twentieth century, Mobile newspapers sometimes hired stenographers and then published precise transcripts, allowing for rich narratives decades later.

As you read *Wicked Mobile*, consider that wickedness is in the eye of the beholder.

In the test of wills between two men who both wanted to be governor of French Louisiana just after Mobile's founding, was it Antoine Laumet de la Mothe, Sieur de Cadillac, or Jean-Baptiste Le Moyne de Bienville who was the rogue? The historical judgment of Mobile is clear: Bienville's name graces the city's most prominent park while Cadillac has been relegated to a mere footnote. But the behavior of both men certainly was wicked enough to qualify for the title.

The Indian sneak attack on a settlement near the Tensaw River northeast of Mobile before Alabama even was a U.S. state may seem to qualify as a no-brainer wicked event. The killing that hot summer day was gruesome. But could wickedness not apply also to the U.S. Army, which earlier had launched an attack on a Creek Indian war party? Or for that matter, what about the commander of Fort Mims, whose lackadaisical attitude and incompetence practically invited the attack?

Then there is the young man hanged for the unprovoked murder of his friend, who was sick with tuberculosis. Clearly wicked.

But what if he was wrongly accused?

Or Raymond and Samuel Dyson, a pair of brothers who beat a man to death inside the elegant Battle House Hotel in downtown Mobile to settle "an affair of honor." Perhaps they committed an evil. Perhaps the evildoer was the victim, who had had an affair with Raymond Dyson's wife.

Can an entire city be wicked?

Mobile during the Prohibition era erected a wall of massive resistance to the ban on alcohol. A city where Mardi Gras and adult beverages long had been an important part of the social fabric fought against efforts by the state of Alabama and later the federal government to impose temperance.

When the ban did become the law, many of Mobile's most prominent citizens participated in the lucrative underground business. The events unfolded much like a southern version of the popular HBO program *Boardwalk Empire*.

Was Mobile wicked or merely fighting the good fight for liberty?

As I said, the answer to these questions often depends on point of view.

This book is not meant to be the first and last word on every misdeed in three hundred years. There are countless others; these are just some of my favorites.

In putting together this book, I was aided enormously by both the subject matter—an old, fascinating city—and some very kind people who know a lot more than I do.

The University of South Alabama Archives has a treasure-trove of historical photographs in its Doy Leale McCall Rare Book and Manuscript Library. If it was a big deal in Mobile, chances are there is a file about it at the Local History and Genealogy section of the Mobile Public Library. All of the librarians were helpful.

Speaking of helpful, Scotty Kirkland, the history curator at the Mobile History Museum, put numerous letters and other primary source materials in my hands and made time and space for me to work. Equally helpful was Johnny Biggs, an archive specialist at the Baldwin County Department of Archives and History. He went above and beyond in helping me find materials.

Collétte King, a semiretired archivist at the Mobile County Probate Court, shared some absolute gems with me during my research.

Little has been published about the Battle House honor killing, and that fascinating chapter in Mobile history likely would have remained mostly forgotten if not for the tenacity of Mobile lawyer Matt Green. He has done more research than anyone on the topic and was kind enough to walk me through those events.

Likewise, my old editor at the *Mobile Press-Register*, Steve Joynt, deserves a great deal of credit for doing the detective work in separating fact from legend in the story of Joe Cain, the godfather of Mobile's Mardi Gras celebration.

Finally, I would like to thank the editors at The History Press, whose patience I tried as I blew up deadlines. My wife, Kerry; daughter, Mariah; and son, Declan, also showed patience, for the many hours I missed at home. My wife and Mariah, age twelve, also gave up their time to help me proofread the manuscript.

Writers are taught to avoid clichés, but there is one that nonetheless applies: I hope you enjoy reading these stories as much as I enjoyed writing them.

Chapter 1

THE WICKED RIVALRIES OF FRENCH MOBILE

In the summer of 1713, a ship carrying twenty-five marriageable young women, French furnishings, servants and the man who had come to take the reins of France's fledging and flailing Louisiana colony arrived off the coast of Dauphin Island.

Antoine Laumet de la Mothe, Sieur de Cadillac, who a dozen years earlier had founded Detroit, had come to claim his spot as governor of Louisiana. He had won the job through a mixture of bravado and deception. Even his name was a con. He had been born Antoine Laumet in the small French village of Gascony between 1656 and 1658, but he called himself Antoine de la Mothe, Sieur de Cadillac, on his marriage certificate.

His father, Jean Laumet, had been a minor provincial judge who had lost the family's wealth paying his brother's debts, and Antoine grew up poor. But in Antoine's retelling, he claimed to be son of Jean de la Mothe, Seigneur de dict lieu de Cadillac, de Launay et Semontel. He also listed the noble name Malenfant for his bourgeois mother, whose real name was Jeanne Péchagut.

Despite a tenure in Detroit that was uneven, at best, Cadillac managed to win the favor of Jérôme Phélypeaux, Comte de Pontchartrain, the secretary of state for the French navy. He appointed Cadillac governor of the Louisiana colony in 1710. Rather than reporting directly to Louisiana as ordered, however, Cadillac returned to Paris. There, he assumed the task of persuading financier Antoine Crozat to underwrite the colony.

Pontchartrain judged Cadillac to be "excellent...for reestablishing in proper form a new country," although in a sign that he was aware of

Antoine Laumet de La Mothe, Sieur de Cadillac, sweet-talked and conned his way into a series of positions, culminating with his appointment as governor of Louisiana in 1710. He did not actually assume his duties until 1713. *Detroit Historical Museum.*

Cadillac's liabilities also acknowledged that he was sending Cadillac to Louisiana to "get rid" of him.

The need for an influx of new capital was great. The French treasury had been drained by the costly War of Spanish Succession, and Louisiana was in the worst shape of any of France's holdings in the New World. In 1710,

Martin D'Artaguiette—a French naval commissioner—reported that the colonists were near starvation.

"There is no more bacon here; we are reduced to slaughtering the bulls that are in this colony since it is not possible to live only on Indian corn," he wrote. "The majority of soldiers are wearing animal skins and this gives the natives a wretched impression of us."

Theft was on the rise and religious observance on the decline. D'Artaguiette pleaded with the government in Paris to send more women to the colony in order to prevent unmarried men from taking up with Indian women.

Crozat reluctantly agreed in August 1712 to assume financial responsibility for Louisiana after Cadillac had seduced him with tales of a vast territory containing fantastic mineral wealth. Crozat was granted a monopoly on colonial trade, and Cadillac signed on to the Company of Louisiana at a 3.5 percent commission on the sale of goods.

If Cadillac believed his own propaganda, he surely was disappointed by what confronted him when the *Baron de la Fauche* landed at Dauphin Island in June 1713 for the new governor to finally assume his duties three years after his appointment. The colony, in truth, was a backwater compared to Cadillac's native France or even the French settlements in Canada and the Great Lakes frontiers, where he had spent much of his adult life. He saw a poor excuse for a garden with a few fig trees, apple trees, pears trees, a single plum tree and thirty feet of vineyards. Commerce was nearly nonexistent. The soil was sandy.

Cadillac appropriated a vacant, two-story house that had belonged to the brother of his predecessor, Jean-Baptiste Le Moyne de Bienville. The surroundings led him to conclude that Louisiana was "not worth a straw at present."

The entirety of the vast colony, which extended hundreds of miles north from present-day Alabama, Mississippi and Louisiana up the Mississippi River, consisted of some 334 people. And Cadillac made it clear that he did not think much of them.

He described the seventy-five pelt traders and slave hunters as a "mass of rapscallions from Canada, a cutthroat set, with no respect for religion, and abandoned in vice to Indian women. They know nothing of cultivating silk, tobacco or indigo, but only corn and vegetables."

Cadillac complained about the colony's lack of morality, its crude and vulgar colonists and the poor military discipline of its two infantry companies.

"There is a woman on Dauphin Island who yields herself to all comers," he wrote.

Even the boys, Cadillac wrote, had Indian mistresses. The one hundred men who made up the infantry were "the dregs of Canada" and spent most of their time in the woods with the Indians, he wrote.

Bienville, who had been governor before Cadillac's appointment, chaffed at the demotion. After all, he had helped his brother, Pierre Le Moyne d'Iberville, found Mobile, the first capital of Louisiana. Iberville landed first on modern-day Dauphin Island, a barrier island in the Gulf of Mexico. He named it Massacre Island after discovering sixty skeletons on the southwest tip of the landmass.

Jean-Baptist Le Moyne, Sieur de Bienville, helped his brother plant France's flag in Louisiana but undermined the crown's choice for his replacement as governor. *Doy Leale McCall Rare Book and Manuscript Library.*

Iberville instructed Bienville to set up a fort farther up Mobile Bay. The Canadian-born explorer set off from Massacre Island and found an Indian tribe twenty-seven miles north. It was there that the colonists built Fort Louis de la Louisiane in 1702. "We call it Mobile," Iberville declared.

Bienville took command of the fort on January 5, 1702. The small settlement was established, but it was not in a secure location, surrounded by Indians and not far from Pensacola to the east, where the Spanish had constructed their own fort a few years earlier.

The French colony was hampered by a system of governance that diffused

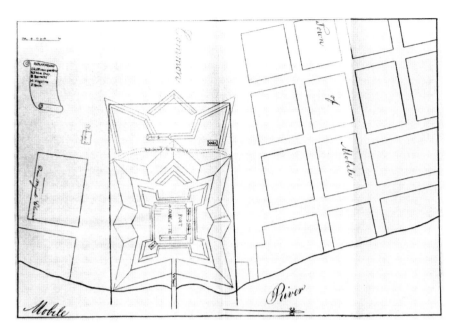

Mobile, even at its new location in 1711, was poorly defended, far from supply lines and surrounded by hostile Indians. It would not be until 1923 that Fort Condé (later called Fort Charlotte under British rule) made the city more secure. *Doy Leale McCall Rare Book and Manuscript Library.*

power among several officials, as well as the tendency of those officials to feud among themselves. As governor, Bienville was the top military authority in the colony. But he had to share power with Nicolas de La Salle, the civilian official.

They did not get along.

La Salle accused Bienville of withholding salaries, speculating in royal property and appropriating public funds. Bienville responded by accusing La Salle of keeping shop like a Jew.

Bienville's relationships with Indian women also drew the ire of the powerful Catholic Church. He called Henri Roulleaux de La Vente—the first pastor of the Mobile parish church—the "most violent, most hot-headed, the blackest-hearted man in the world."

Reports by D'Artaguiette, sent by the minister of the French navy to assist with an inquest into the affairs of the Le Moyne brothers—including suspicions about how Bienville had gained his wealth—had helped prompt the leadership change.

But the French government had decided to leave Bienville in Mobile as Cadillac's deputy in hopes that the new governor would benefit from his experience. It would prove to be just one of the many mistakes made by the French government that would doom its early efforts to build a thriving colony that could rival the British holdings in the New World.

Reporting the king's desires, Pontchartrain wrote that Bienville was to acquaint Cadillac "with all the affairs of the colony. He is convinced that he will do so in good faith."

In a letter to Bienville in 1710, Pontchartrain wrote that the king "desires that you stay on good terms with the governor and give this your greatest attention in order to deserve the favors that His Majesty might grant you when you have vindicated yourself against all the changes that have been leveled at you."

In Bienville's response in June of that year, the deposed essentially said that the crown would not be able to find a replacement better than himself.

"I venture to predict to you that when I am relieved of the burden of civil administration, no one will better govern the colony or (more skillfully) manage the savages," he wrote.

Mobile in 1711 was the capital city of the fledgling French Louisiana colony, a struggling outpost where a few hundred souls barely eked out a living. *Doy Leale McCall Rare Book and Manuscript Library.*

It soon become clear that Cadillac held his predecessor in low regard. In letters to his superiors, he called Bienville a simpleton and fool, and the colony he had governed a "monster which had neither head nor tail."

For Bienville, the feeling was mutual. He already was disappointed that he had been removed as governor of Louisiana and was predisposed to resist Cadillac anyway. The new governor's attitude made that dislike deeply personal.

Bienville refused to marry Cadillac's daughter, a union that might have solidified the relationship. Instead, Bienville tried to undermine Cadillac at every turn. The relationship grew so toxic that Cadillac in 1716 ordered Bienville to make war with the strong Indian nation of Natchez, hoping that he either would fail or be killed. But Bienville returned victorious and earned laurels, further enraging Cadillac.

An investigator had been sent from France to look into allegations that Bienville was pilfering supplies from the king's storehouse and stealing gifts meant to buy goodwill among the Indians. However, Cadillac became convinced that the investigator was not pursuing the case aggressively enough, and he wrote to the crown to complain in 1713.

Cadillac and Bienville sent a torrent of letters to Paris hurling accusations at one another. Cadillac also accused the *ordonnateur*, or director, Jean-Baptiste du Bois Du Clos, Sieur de Montigny, of selling food from the garrison for his own profit. He accused them of conspiring against him and circumventing the monopoly. That killed a promotion the Pontchartrain was going to give Bienville.

Cadillac's brief tenure as governor consisted of one disaster after another. He spent many futile months away from the colony searching Illinois for the silver and other minerals he was convinced it had in abundance. Cadillac spent most of his time in Illinois in a Kaskaskia Indian village, where he tested samples brought by European traders and Indians. But all he discovered was a lead mine near the Saline River.

Despite the meager findings, Cadillac pretended upon his return from an expedition in 1715 to have scored a big win. Louisiana, he wrote, was "a country of gold and silver mines." Although utterly false, the news caused unrest in Mexico.

Cadillac also organized a failed expedition to the Rio Grande and Red River. Du Clos opposed it because he believed it would provoke a Spanish reaction. The only reason the colonists agreed to participate, he wrote, was to escape their miserable condition.

Cadillac agreed to make participants pay for the journey, themselves, in order to limit Crozat's risk.

"I have undertaken that enterprise at the expense and cost of the party," he wrote.

Crozat fronted the expedition party supplies on the condition that the explorers reimburse the company and give it a monopoly on the trade they established with Mexico. Most returned a few months later, however, unable to reach Mexico because of wars that were raging in the area. Expedition leader Louis Juchereau Saint-Denis, meanwhile, did reach the Spanish outpost of the Rio Grande in 1714. But he was betrothed to the granddaughter of the garrison's commandant and then he was held in semi-captivity in Mexico. He wrote to Cadillac in September 1715 to report his intention of leading a Spanish expedition to the Red River.

Cadillac, thus, had failed. And Crozat was forced to absorb the loss of his investment.

When he was in Mobile, Cadillac feuded with other colonial officials, roiled the colonists and harmed relations with the Indians. The colonists, many of whom were Canadian, sided with Bienville and Du Clos. They openly ridiculed Cadillac, nicknaming him the "Black Prince" because the colony's slaves were convinced he was of African descent and because he boasted that an ancestor had entertained a black prince at his home.

The infighting polarized the colony and eroded military discipline. Planned overtures to neighboring Indian tribes routinely were postponed amid Cadillac's indecision, and fortification of the military installation was put off. Du Clos began to neglect his duties out of spite, and the inhabitants lost confidence in the colonial government. Some even talked of joining the British colonies.

Cadillac accused Bienville of refusing his order to occupy the Natchez territory; Bienville countered that the order was impossible because Cadillac had refused to provide reinforcements. Cadillac forbade Bienville from erecting forts in Natchez and sent him only forty untrained recruits. He told Bienville to scatter the men "in the dwelling of the savages" in order to avoid "useless expense."

The two clashed over policy. Bienville favored expanding the colony to the Lower Ohio and Natchez Rivers. But Cadillac considered it unwise to spread the population too thin.

"It will be necessary sooner or later to come back to my point of view which has been to think, at the outset only of fortifying Dauphin Island, in order to conserve our port, our ships, the merchandise, and the inhabitants," he wrote in 1716.

Cadillac undid much of Bienville's skillful diplomacy in building good relations with the Indians, ignoring his lieutenant governor's advice. Cadillac offended the Indians to such an extent that the colony's Indian alliances were in a state of collapse by the end of 1714.

Cadillac fared no better in his diplomacy with the British colonies. The governor of Carolina, Charles Craven, rejected Cadillac's suggestion for creating zones of influences among the Indians. Cadillac denounced Craven, at one point issuing idle threats in a futile effort to force the return of slaves that had been kidnapped from French allies.

Relations finally improved after Cadillac left for a mineral-hunting expedition in Illinois and delegated responsibility for Indian affairs to the more capable Bienville. He was aided by Du Clos, who gave Bienville the funds that he had denied Cadillac.

But Indian relations soured again when Cadillac returned from his Illinois expedition at the end of 1715 and resumed control.

Although Cadillac's administration was no help, many of the colony's problems were beyond his control. By 1713, pay had been frozen for six years, causing unrest among the troops. Crozat assumed future obligations, not past debts.

Conditions were perpetually bad. The colony suffered from a shortage of useful workers because the skills of many who made the journey—from ribbon makers to weavers—were of little utility on the frontier. Many pretended to be tradesmen in the hopes of a salary boost.

In 1713, workers on Dauphin Island found themselves stranded without lodging or food and lived for weeks on shellfish.

Women sent to populate the colony had bad reputations and poor looks. Families in France refused to give up their best young women. Extreme poverty in Louisiana made married life difficult. Some women married soldiers barely able to support themselves, let alone families.

Many colonists refused to marry the French girls, preferring to sleep with Indian women and lead seminomadic lives.

Throughout Cadillac's tenure, the colony remained small, with a stagnant population. Profits were mediocre. The military force was no more than sixty men, and discipline was poor. A 1715 census pegged the colony's population at 215 people. Cadillac and other officials provided vague and contradictory estimates of the civilian population.

Agriculture was limited to Dauphin Island, a small region near Fowl River, and an area around Mobile filled with trees and stumps. It was tough going even in those areas, as colonists labored against drought, humidity and bad soil. A merchant named Baron offered a negative assessment of Mobile and Dauphin Island after visiting in 1714.

"The bottom of the soil of both establishments is hardly worth anything," he wrote. "This is simply a bed of sand that one tries not at all to dig."

Cadillac showed a propensity to flout the rules. He ignored the king's restrictions on land grants and gave away titles "at will." When Crozat preferred to wring as much profit as possible out of the colony, at the expense of building and strengthening the settlement, Cadillac responded by encouraging illegal trade with Spanish Pensacola.

The colonists secretly traded maize in Pensacola and even exchanged goods with the British, with whom the French frequently warred.

Cadillac also never seemed to figure out the proper relationship with the colony's religious faction. His hostility toward the Jesuits predated his arrival in Louisiana, and he vacillated in the colony between allying himself with the missionaries and thinking them overly severe.

A missionary named Françoise Le Maire filed unflattering reports about both Cadillac and Bienville. Bienville, he contended, was guilty of intercepting merchandise arriving from the interior, to the detriment of the impoverished colonists.

Meanwhile, he wrote, Cadillac was "a man without faith, without religion, without honor, and without conscience."

———•———

There ought to have been plenty of red flags from Cadillac's career in Detroit.

Before founding the city, he became a seaman under François Guyon, his future wife's uncle. After serving as an infantry captain in Canada, he went to Port Royal, now Annapolis Royal, in Nova Scotia. He returned to Canada and in 1687 married Marie Therese Guyon in Quebec.

The following year, Cadillac was granted land in Maine. In 1690, he spent time in the court of King Louis XIV, living on borrowed money. While he was away, the British sacked his home in Maine.

Aided by the cache that came from marrying into the prominent Guyon family, Cadillac took command of Fort Michilimackinac, the most important French possession in western Canada.

The Jesuits at Mackinac opposed trading liquor to the Indians, but Cadillac reasoned that if they did not sell rum, the English would. He told the Jesuits that their conduct "smelled of sedition a hundred years old." He disliked the "sweet smelling odor of sanctity" of aristocrats.

Cadillac resorted to devious tactics to keep Canadian settlers from leaving the remote outpost. For instance, he refused to provide escorts through hostile Indian lands. He struck a covert deal with the Miami tribe: They were free to plunder any French parties without "mark of permission," as long as they did not kill their victims. The Indians were to force travelers back to the fort.

Cadillac claimed he had no authority to issue "passports," smugly suggesting that it was safer to remain inside the fort.

In 1701, he moved the garrison to Fort Detroit and proposed building a colony that would prevent the British from challenging the French position in North America. Cadillac made a fortune in the fur trade in the Great Lakes region. But as it would the following decade in Mobile, his personality inspired dissension and infighting there. When complaints reached Pontchartrain in the first decade of the eighteenth century, he sent François Clairambault d'Aigremont to investigate. His report filed in 1708 was not kind.

Aigremont found Cadillac's administration to be "incoherent, inefficient, self-interested, and marred by his difficulties with religious orders." He wrote that Cadillac's rule was tyrannical and was despised by French settlers and Indians, alike. Cadillac required tradesmen to pay him large sums for the right to work. A jug of brandy, which cost two to four livres in Canada, went for twenty livres in Detroit.

Far from the prosperous and thriving colony Cadillac had depicted in reports to Paris, Detroit appeared to Aigremont to be a struggling outpost. Besides the soldiers and a few hundred Indians, Detroit had just sixty-two settlers.

In 1706 and 1707, the Hurons, Ottawas and Miamis who settled near Detroit nearly went to war. Aigremont blamed Cadillac.

Aigremont's assessment would foreshadow many of the same difficulties Cadillac would face in Louisiana.

———•———

By 1716, the French government had had enough of Cadillac's leadership and recalled him to France for "lack of intelligence" and failure to grow the colony.

Crozat also wanted out. In January 1717, he petitioned for an end to his monopoly and on August 23 became free of his obligations to the colony.

"My three principal projects: discovery of mines of gold and silver, the establishment and maintenance of workers for plantations of tobacco, commerce with Spain were dissipated," he wrote in his petition.

A Scottish financier and petty gambler of Scottish descent named John Law formed the Company of the West and won trade rights to the colony. He had founded a bank in Paris and issued paper money backed partially by fraudulent assets. He also received a twenty-five-year monopoly on the beaver trade in Canada.

The duke of Orleans turned over almost total control of the colony's finances, and Law launched a worldwide advertising campaign to lure colonists to Louisiana. The efforts included colorful posters advertising the colony as a paradise.

The duplicity might have been taken straight from Cadillac's playbook, but perhaps after three mostly miserable years in the struggling colony, Cadillac sought to set the record straight. He publicly disputed Law's claims.

One month after Cadillac's return to France, the government tossed him and his eldest son into the infamous Bastille prison on September 27, 1717, on charges of "having made improper statements against the government of France and the colonies."

A little more than four months later, he was freed and granted the Cross of St. Louis and back salary as a consolation but retained no influence in national government. He retired to his native Gascony, bought the governorship of Castelsarrasin in 1723 and died there in obscurity seven years later.

Bienville, meanwhile, went on to found New Orleans in 1718. It became the provincial capital in 1722 and, ultimately, one of America's most celebrated cities. He also got two more stints as Louisiana governor. Controversy dogged him, however. He captured Pensacola from the Spanish and in 1724 wrote the colony's "black code," regulating the conduct of African slaves.

That same year, the government recalled him to France and stripped him of office. He returned to office in 1733, receiving "a welcome of joy and satisfaction without parallel."

As for Law, his company gave up its interest in Louisiana in 1731, and it reverted to a royal colony.

Mobile would see better days.

Chapter 2

The Massacre at Fort Mims

The sound of drums announcing the noon mealtime in crowded Fort Mims also was the signal for some two hundred Creek Indian warriors who had been hiding all morning in thick vegetation close to the hastily constructed stockade.

The warriors now sprinted toward the wide-open eastern gates, swiftly but silently, war clubs, tomahawks and a few rifles in hand.

The date was August 30, 1813. Although several hundred area settlers and soldiers had holed up inside the fort more than a month earlier for protection against rumored Indian attacks, the defenders could hardly have been less prepared. The outer gate on the western side of the stockade was unbolted, and both gates on the eastern side were open. The soldiers were hungover after a night of whiskey and whimsy.

The sentry charged with watching the horizon for signs of Indians instead was looking over his shoulder at a card game. He did not spot the invading force until the warriors were thirty steps away. When he finally did spy them, it was too late.

"Indians!" the guard yelled, shooting his musket in the air. "The Indians! The Indians!" The warning set off panicked confusion in the camp. Men scurried for their weapons. Major Daniel Beasley, the man in command of the fort's defenses, raced to shut the massive outer gate. But it had been open for weeks, and rainstorms that frequently batter the Mobile area during the summer months had pushed a wall of dirt against the gate.

Because of the poor leadership of the top military officer inside Fort Mims, the settlers were completely unprepared for the Indian attack when it came. *Doy Leale McCall Rare Book and Manuscript Library.*

Unable to budge it, Beasley quickly found a horde of Indians upon him and suffered a gunshot or a blow to the stomach from a spiked war club. Trampled and dazed, Beasley managed to crawl behind the gate and yell to his men to make a stand just before he died.

The ensuing battle raged all day long. When it was over, it had become the bloodiest massacre of American civilians in U.S. history up to that point. Hundreds on both sides died, and the conquering Creeks brutally bludgeoned women and children among the survivors, and claimed some 250 scalps as trophies.

A *Mobile Daily Register* article in 1884 recounted the massacre from the perspective of a 105-year-old black man named Tony Morgan, who claimed to have been a slave of Judge Harry Toulmin. He told the newspaper that he was inside the fort at the time of the attack. He recalled an officer from Fort Stoddert warning of an imminent Indian attack.

That warning, according to the newspaper, went unheeded.

"After the entrance of the Indians into the fort, the most horrible butchery was committed," the article states. "Men, women and children were brained without mercy by the Indians using tomahawks."

———•———

Fort Mims started simply as the home of Samuel Mims, a Virginian who had come by way of North Carolina to what eventually would become the Mississippi Territory. He had spent some time in Creek country, loosely confederated tribes with a combined population of eighteen to twenty-four thousand over much of what now is Alabama and western Georgia.

Mims left after the decline of the deerskin trade, signed an oath to the Spanish crown in 1787 and, the following January, married Hannah Raines of St. Augustine in a Catholic wedding.

A decade of land speculation along the Tombigbee River and the northern edge of the city of Mobile made him wealthy. In 1797, Mims acquired 524 acres near Boatyard Lake close to the modern-day village of Stockton, about thirty-five miles northeast of Mobile.

A Spanish census shows him to have had 150 barrels of maize, sixteen slaves, ten horses, ninety cattle and one hundred pounds of tobacco in 1786. The following year, his holdings had grown to 250 barrels of maize.

While overseeing slave plantations, he also went into the ferry business. It became quite lucrative after Congress created the Mississippi Territory in 1798 and authorized the construction of Fort Stoddert in Mount Vernon, north of Mobile, in 1799. That made the ferry crossings of Mims and Adam Hollinger the preferred route across the Delta for westbound pioneers. Benjamin Hawkins, the principal U.S. representative to the Creek Indians, issued up to one hundred passes a month to pioneer families.

As the population of white settlers grew, relations with the neighboring Indians soured. During the 1780s and 1790s, Creek warriors raided settlers' plantations, stealing horses and slaughtering cattle.

By 1804, the region numbered some two hundred pioneer families, including fifty to sixty on the east side, known as the Tensaw settlement. President Thomas Jefferson's public lands commissioner, Ephraim Kirby, held the settlers in low regard. In a report to Washington, D.C., he wrote that the inhabitants, with few exceptions, were "illiterate, wild and savage, of depraved morals unworthy of public confidence or private esteem, litigious, disunited, and knowing each other, universally distrustful of each other."

The administration of justice, in Kirby's words, was "imbecile and corrupt," and the militia was "without discipline or competent officers."

Recent arrivals from the States "are almost universally fugitives from justice, and many of them felons of the first magnitude."

Circumstances, however, eventually would force these ragtag settlers together. Indian raids over the next decade grew, as did sentiment within the Creek nation for an all-out war to expel the white interlopers.

In response to the threat of violence, Mims built a palisade compound around his home. Toulmin, the superior court judge for the Tombigbee District of the Mississippi Territory, wrote on July 23, 1813, of the panic gripping the region: "The people have been fleeing all night."

The conflict reached a boiling point in the summer of 1813. A band of Creek warriors obtained guns from their Spanish allies in Pensacola, alarming the Americans. U.S. officials decided to launch a preemptive strike; forces took the Indians by surprise during their mealtime at Burnt Corn Creek on July 26.

The confrontation ended with a retreat of American forces, but not before they inflicted serious damage on the Indian war party. Reports of American atrocities enraged the Creek nation, prompting the Redstick warriors to return to Pensacola and rearm.

That month, some 400 to 550 people crowded into Fort Mims. They included settlers and about 100 slaves, as well as soldiers from the Mississippi Territorial Volunteers and the local Tensaw militia—plus fifty or more children and dozens of dogs. Samuel Mims was sixty-six at the time.

The settlers and the Creek Indians were closely intertwined. The fort's residents included friendly Indians and mixed-race people with Indian and white parents. These so-called métis had friends and relatives among the Redsticks who launched the attack.

Conditions were cramped. The entire compound was only one and a quarter acres. It included seventeen buildings, among them an unfinished blockhouse on the southwest corner and a log palisade. About twenty white métis families lived in hastily constructed log cabins. Mims and his family shared their house and possessions.

The soldiers, meanwhile, lived in tents along the northern and eastern double walls.

Outhouses, rows of bee gums (beehives made from hollow trees), cabins and shelters covered the rest of the space.

In the center was the Mims house, itself, a single-story frame structure, unusually expensive for the time.

The mass of people and animals living in close quarters for weeks led to illness, the primary treatment of which was an extra gill (equal to a quarter of a pint) of whiskey and bleeding. Weeks without Indian sightings, combined with shrinking supplies, helped contribute to the complacency that fully enveloped the camp by the day of the attack. Some settlers began leaving the fort to search for wild berries. Others returned to their farms or bought food from those with extra supplies.

In retrospect, the men charged with defending Fort Mims had plenty of warning of an imminent attack. General Ferdinand Claiborne, the commander of Fort Stoddert, inspected Fort Mims on August 7 and found its readiness wanting. He ordered Beasley to fortify the pickets and build more blockhouses, an order that apparently went unheeded.

In the days leading up to the attack, Beasley received several reports of Indian sightings but chose to discount them.

A slave of Zachariah McGirth named Jo—one of three captured and interrogated by the Redstick Indian force—escaped and carried warnings to Fort Mims. Beasley gave them no credence.

A pair of slave boys reported seeing Indians on August 29, the day before the attack. But when a patrol sent by Beasley turned up no signs of the Creeks, the commander ordered one of the boys whipped. The following morning that same boy and a slave owned by settler John Randon reported seeing Redsticks within a mile of the fort as they were tending to cattle.

A scout, James Cornells, rode to the east gate on the morning of August 30 and shouted to Beasley that he had seen thirteen Indians in the woods a short distance from the fort. Beasley—who Cornells later recalled appeared to be drunk—said Cornells must have seen a gang of red cattle.

"That gang of red cattle will give you a hell of a kick before night," Cornells replied.

Beasley ordered Cornells arrested, but he avoided apprehension by riding off for Fort Pierce.

Inside Fort Mims, men sat in two circles discussing what they might do if an Indian attack did come. Someone played the fiddle. Beasley oversaw the flogging of Randon's slave, who had reported danger.

Josiah Fletcher, the owner of another slave who had reported seeing Indians, believed the man. He refused to allow Beasley to discipline him, prompting the angry major to order Fletcher and his family to leave the fort by ten o'clock the next day. Reluctantly, Fletcher backed down and allowed the slave to receive a lash.

Again spotting Indians after he was sent out to herd cattle on the morning of the attack, Randon's slave fled for Fort Pierce rather than risk another beating.

At ten o'clock that morning—two hours before the assault—Beasley sent his final dispatch to Fort Stoddert. In it, he reported 106 soldiers of the First Regiment of the Mississippi Territorial Volunteers, including 6 on leave to Mobile. The defense also included 41 or 42 militiamen.

Beasley declared his men fit for duty and expressed no concern for the preparedness of the fort, even as hundreds of Redsticks at that moment were surrounding the compound in secret. He alluded to the reported Indian sighting but dismissed it.

"Sir, I send enclosed morning reports of my command," the dispatch states. "I have improved the fort at this place and made it much stronger than when you were here…There was a false alarm yesterday…But the alarm proved to be false."

Beasley boasted of his ability "to maintain the fort against any number of Indians."

———•———

Responsibility for drawing up the battle plan on the Creek side fell to William Weatherford, a strapping man in his thirties who had grown up with one foot in the Indian world and another in the white one. His mother, Sehoy III, was a member of the influential Wind clan of the Creek people. His father, Charles Weatherford, was a red-haired Scotsman who had ridden into the Upper Creek territory with Samuel Mims in 1779 or early 1780 to escape the Revolutionary War.

Creek society was matrilineal, meaning inheritance and family identity passed through mothers, not fathers. By marrying Sehoy, Charles Weatherford gained a measure of status. He participated in Creek council meetings and trafficked in stolen horses and slaves.

In Creek society, because of the matrilineal structure, maternal uncles shared closer bonds with children than the biological fathers. As a result, Creek Indian chief Alexander McGillivray played an important role in William Weatherford's upbringing. By 1787, McGillivray owned a thriving plantation in the community of Little River, situated in the northernmost section of Baldwin County, Alabama.

Charles Weatherford spent a year in a Spanish jail in New Orleans over an unpaid debt and subsequently sought to undermine Spanish rule and McGillivray's own diplomacy. After McGillivray's death in 1793, Charles Weatherford worked to promote stronger Creek ties with the United States.

Weatherford in 1803 helped Benjamin Hawkins, the U.S. government agent in the Creek territories, apprehend British loyalist William Augustus Bowles, who had attempted to lead the Creeks to form an autonomous Muskogee nation. William Weatherford assisted in the capture when Bowles tried to address the National Creek Council at Hickory Ground.

William Weatherford thus had divided loyalties. But he held deeply to the traditionalist religious beliefs espoused by the prophets who urged violent confrontation with the Americans and turned away from his European side.

William Weatherford, whose father was Scottish and mother was Creek Indian, planned the attack on Fort Mims in 1813. *Doy Leale McCall Rare Book and Manuscript Library.*

Until the day he died in 1824, Weatherford regretted his role in the attack on the fort, which housed some of his own relatives. He had worked to limit the carnage that would result from the sneak attack.

"Tomorrow, I will lead you into battle," he told his men on the eve of the attack. "I go to fight warriors, not squaws. A Creek warrior gains no merit in spilling the blood of a squaw. The women and children should be spared. They can be carried back to the nation and serve the red man as servants."

If Weatherford was a reluctant warrior, however, he held nothing back as a tactician. The successful attack caused his legend to grow over the ensuing decades. According to an 1858 letter by an acquaintance, Thomas S. Woodward, Weatherford went by the war name Hopnicafutsahia—Truth

One hundred years after the massacre at Fort Mims, Alabama commemorated the event with a historical marker. *Doy Leale McCall Rare Book and Manuscript Library.*

Maker or Teller. Another moniker was Billy Larney, which translates to "Yellow Billy."

In 1855, decades after Weatherford's death, he acquired yet another name—Lamochattee, or Red Eagle. The work *The Red Eagle: A Poem of the South* sprang from the pen of Alexander Beaufort Meek, a lawyer and accomplished chess player who one day would become Alabama's attorney general.

Some historical accounts of the Massacre of Fort Mims refer to Weatherford by this name, but modern historians have indicated that he likely never went by that title in life.

Weatherford's battle plan called for sending an initial wave of two hundred warriors through the open eastern gate, and while they occupied the settlers' defense, following up with additional forces assaulting the fort from the west, south and north.

The Redsticks gained valuable intelligence from the three captured slaves, who indicated the fort's commanders believed there was no threat of an

Indian invasion. Weatherford harbored doubts that the defenses could be so lax and stole close to the fort to have a look for himself.

Convinced that the fort, indeed, was ripe for assault, Weatherford rode toward Boatyard Lake after midnight and took up position about three quarters of a mile from the fort.

On the morning of August 30, the women in the stockade began preparing breakfast and the scent of frying bacon and biscuits wafted into the warm, humid air. Two hundred Redstick warriors under the command of Peter McQueen made their way to a ravine about two hundred yards from the gate and waited for the signal to attack.

The men, some painted red and black and naked except for their loincloths, took the fort by surprise. Nehemiah Page, a Territorial Mississippi Volunteer who was sleeping off a hangover in the horse stables outside the fort, saw the approaching warriors and watched through a gap in the wood.

"It is impossible to imagine people so horribly painted," Dr. Thomas Holmes, the fort's assistant surgeon, later recounted.

Page ducked out of sight until the Indian invaders had passed him and then jumped out of the stable and ran for his life toward the Alabama River. A little dog that had come with the Indians turned after seeing Page and then started running after him. Reaching the river, Page dove into the water, the dog closely behind him. The dog, sometimes in his wake, sometimes at his head, helped Page reach the other side. Exhausted, he finally made it to the safety of the white settlements.

After that, Page would never leave the dog's side.

Inside the fort, meanwhile, four feather-clad Indians chosen by the prophet Paddy Walsh sprinted past the fallen Major Daniel Beasley and swung their clubs without fear or mercy. They had been told by Walsh that they were impervious to the white man's bullets. Walsh had predicted that no more than three Creek warriors would die that day.

The Redsticks were not immune to bullets, however, and three of the four quickly died. The fourth, Nahomahteeathle Hopoie, retreated.

Under loud war whoops, the battle was on. Redstick warriors poured through the eight-foot-wide gate and engaged soldiers in fierce hand-to-hand combat as bodies piled up. Between the inner and outer gates, half of the Mississippi Territorial Volunteers died within the first few minutes of the battle.

Dixon Bailey, the commander of the Tensaw militiamen, rushed toward Tenskwatawa, the Shawnee prophet, and shot him dead. His men hacked the fallen Indian to pieces.

As the battle raged, Weatherford blew a whistle hanging from his neck, a signal for the second wave to begin. Warriors advanced on all sides and fired a sustained barrage of arrows and bullets at the fort. The attackers were able to easily seize most of the portholes meant for the fort's soldiers to fire at the invaders from safety.

This was because of one of the many deficiencies of the fort. The portholes were only three and a half feet above the ground, without a protective ditch or bank. A properly designed fort would have placed them much higher, putting them out of reach from the other side and allowing defenders to fire from an elevated position. Instead, the Creeks seized the advantage, using those portholes to fire inside the fort. At times, both militiamen and Indians jammed guns inside the same holes and fired simultaneously.

Mississippi Territorial Volunteers Captain C. Hatton Middleton led a counterattack at the east gate while Captain William Jack defended the pickets on the southern side. During the fierce fighting at the gate, Middleton and most of his men perished. Jack, too, died early in the fighting.

The fort's women took up the defense, loading muskets and rifles and handing them to the remaining men. According to an account by nineteenth-century lawyer and historian Albert James Pickett, "The women now animated the men to defend them, by assisting in loading the guns."

Indians attacking from the west side found the inner gate barred shut. They scaled the wall and took over the unprotected blockhouse on the southwest corner of the fort.

Directing the assault from the northern wall, Weatherford sent 150 Creek warriors at Bailey's men, who offered the fort's stiffest resistance. The Redsticks would dive to the ground, reload and spring to their feet to fire.

Bailey, himself a métis, knew that Creeks historically fought only in short spurts and reasoned that he could defend the fort if he and his men could manage to hold out long enough.

By 2:00 p.m., the Creeks and settlers had been fighting for two hours. In the bastion, where Bailey's men had holed up, blood was shoe deep. Some three hundred Indians had died mostly along the north side portholes.

The Redsticks withdrew and convened a council at the cabin of a Mrs. O'Neal on the Federal Road northeast of the fort. The participants elected Weatherford to take over for the Far-off Warrior, Hopoie Tastanagi (or Hopvye Tustunuke). A debate ensued over whether the Creeks had sufficiently humbled the settlers or whether they should return and go for total destruction.

During the lull, soldiers at the fort hit the whiskey barrel.

After about an hour, the Redsticks renewed the battle, this time launching flaming arrows into the fort. The roof of the smokehouse caught fire, as did the roof of the kitchen and other nearby structures. Indian warriors chopped down the western gate.

James and Daniel Bailey, brothers of Tensaw militia commander Dixon Bailey, went with other men to the attic of the Mims house—the highest point in the compound—and rained gunfire at the Creeks in the fields north and south of the fort.

Wave after wave of Redsticks charged Patrick's Loomhouse, a still intact building on the property, stumbling over the corpses of fallen comrades. Thwarted, the remaining men broke off the attack and joined Creek warriors elsewhere in the fort.

The back gate fell, and Weatherford led a group of warriors into the fort. Susannah Hatterway, the Creek wife of one of the American settlers, later reported watching Weatherford gracefully leap over a pile of logs nearly as tall as his six-foot-two frame. He shouted, "Dixon Bailey, today one or both of us must die."

Now five hours old, the battle continued among the exhausted combatants. The Indian fighters continued to launch flaming arrows at the Mims house, where most of the women and children had gone. As the structure caught fire, their screams rose above the war whoops. The fire-weakened roof finally collapsed, dragging the Bailey brothers to their deaths and crushing dozens of women and children inside.

In 1847, Dr. Holmes recalled the horror and carnage from that bloody afternoon three decades earlier. "The way that many of the unfortunate women were mangled and cut to pieces is shocking to humanity, for very many of the women who were pregnant had their unborn infants cut from the womb and lay by their bleeding mothers," he wrote.

Survivors headed toward the bastion. An account by historian Albert James Pickett in 1851 put it this way: "Soon it was full to overflowing. The weak, wounded, and feeble were pressed to death and trodden under foot. The spot presented the appearance of one immense mass of human beings, herded together too close to defend themselves, and, like beeves in the slaughter pen of the butcher, a prey to those who fired upon them."

Frenzied Redstick warriors slaughtered the armed and helpless, alike, with tomahawks and knives. David Mims, Samuel's seventy-six-year-old brother, fell from a powerful blow from a club, which opened a large hole in his head. Gushing blood, with one of his last breaths, he said, "Oh God, I am a dead man."

An Indian warrior lifted his head and cut his scalp.

Dixon Bailey, concluding that the battle was lost, now urged people to try to escape. "All is lost," he said. "My family are to be butchered."

Fire spread from building to building. The powder magazine exploded, sending debris and ash into the sky.

A few of the remaining settlers made it through a gap in the pickets, but most died. Indian warriors killed some of the people who did manage to flee the fort. The assistant surgeon, Dr. Holmes—who also was a private in the Mississippi Territorial Volunteers—fled with a slave named Tom carrying Dixon Bailey's severely ill teenage son. The slave turned around and returned to the fort, handing over the boy to the Creek warriors, who killed him with a knife.

Thirteen soldiers intended to make a stand in the open to help civilians escape, but they scattered under heavy fire.

A slave woman named Hester made it to Fort Stoddert and gave the first account of the massacre.

Children and women lay in mangled heaps. Redstick warriors stripped and scalped the women and dismembered the victims. They cut unborn children from their mothers. A soldier named Rushbury reportedly died from fright.

Creek warriors questioned Dixon Bailey's sister, who pointed to James Dixon's body and said, "I am the sister of that great man you have murdered there."

The warriors then knocked her down, cut her open and emptied her insides. They threw some of the corpses, as well as some of the wounded, into the fire.

Susannah Hatterway took four-year-old Elizabeth Randon in one hand and a young slave girl in the other and led the terrified children into the open.

"Let us go out and be killed together," she said.

Efa Tastanagi, the so-called Dog Warrior, recognized Hatterway as a woman who had been like a surrogate mother to him. He stepped in front of a group of fellow Creek warriors and prevented them from killing the woman and children.

Weatherford's half-brother, David Tate, later told his son-in-law, "As soon as he was satisfied…that the Fort would fall…he rode off, as he had not the heart to witness what he knew would follow, to wit, the indiscriminate slaughter of the inmates for the Fort."

Just before five o'clock in the afternoon, the killing finally stopped. The Creek warriors took Hatterway and the two girls, along with other women and children, prisoner. The bounty included about one hundred captured settlers, two hundred or more scalps, horses and other property.

Half of the Indian force, however, lay dead, disabled or wounded.

The blockhouse and adjacent sections of pickets were the only parts of the fort that escaped the fire. Days later, U.S. troops buried 247 bodies at the fort. Major Joseph P. Kennedy, in a report to General Claiborne, described the toll: "Indians, negroes, white men, women, and children lay in one promiscuous ruin. All were scalped, and the families of every age, were butchered in a manner which is neither decent nor language will permit me to describe."

The brazen attack heightened alarm throughout the region. Fearing another Indian assault, authorities evacuated women at Fort Stoddert to Mobile. Judge Toulmin, who could see signs of the battle from the safety of that installation, offered a highly critical assessment of Beasley's performance.

The battle inside Fort Mims raged until near five o'clock in the afternoon. By then, hundreds on both side lay dead or wounded, and most of the buildings inside the compound had been destroyed. *Doy Leale McCall Rare Book and Manuscript Library.*

"It was but this morning that Major Beasley wrote down that he believed that the indications of the approach of Indians, of which he had recvd. on account, was unfounded and at noon he was vigorously assailed at Fort Mims on Tensaw by a considerable body of them," Toulmin wrote on the evening of August 30. "What the result is we do not know, but the smoke of burning houses in that quarter are now seen on the river bank at Fort Stoddert."

In the aftermath of the fighting, General Claiborne praised Beasley's bravery and that of his men.

"Never [have] men fought better," he wrote.

But Claiborne also wrote that "such was the advantage given to the enemy, by neglecting the most obvious precautions, all their bravery was thrown away...Had the gates been kept closed, and the men properly posted...all experience shows that such a force might have kept at bay a thousand Indians."

The Creek victory at Fort Mims was a costly one. Historians estimate more than half of the Redstick warriors died during the battle; many others would later succumb to wounds they suffered during the fight.

More importantly, it sparked the Creek Indian War, which ended with the Indian defeat at Horseshoe Bend on March 27, 1814, by the superior American Army led by Major General Andrew Jackson. That battle followed a string of victories that Jackson rang up at Tallassee, Talladega, Hillabee and Tallaseehatchee.

The Redsticks surrendered with the Treaty of Fort Jackson on August 9, 1814, forfeiting forty thousand square miles to the Americans. It was a prelude to one of the darkest chapters in American history, the forced relocation known as the "Trail of Tears" of tens of thousands of Indians to lands west of the Mississippi River.

The assault on Fort Mims had convinced many Americans that peaceful cohabitation among the Indian tribes in the western territories was impossible.

Speaking for many of his countrymen, Jackson said, "We must hasten to the frontier, or we shall find it drenched with the blood of our citizens."

Chapter 3

THE MURDERER AND THE OAK TREE

At half past one o'clock in the afternoon on February 20, 1835, the jailer rapped on the door of the cell where Charles R.S. Boyington had spent the last nine months chained to a wall. The young man had been dreading this day ever since a Mobile County judge sentenced him on November 29, 1834, to die for the brutal slaying of his friend and roommate, Nathaniel Frost.

Even as the jailer led him to the procession that would carry him to his death, Boyington held out faint hope that he might yet somehow avoid his fate. He asked the jailer if the governor, perhaps, had arrived.

He had not.

Boyington had spent the previous two and a half hours in conversation and prayer with Reverend William T. Hamilton, pastor of Government Street Presbyterian Church, who had spent several mostly fruitless months trying to persuade the condemned man to atone and accept God.

Boyington wrote a letter to his mother and another one to his brother.

Then it was time to march, more than an hour from the big iron gates on the St. Emanuel Street side of the jail north to Government Street, west to St. Charles Street then south a little past Church Street through the area known at the time as Buzzards Roost for the birds that would swoop down for the scraps left by the neighborhood's butchers.

The route had been chosen so Boyington would have to pass by the spot where Frost's badly mangled and bloody body had been found the previous May. It was just outside the cemetery where Boyington soon would be buried.

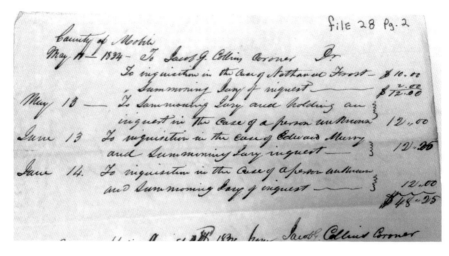

This is a document related to the coroner's inquest into the murder of Nathaniel Frost in 1834. *Mobile County Probate Court records.*

Boyington made no last-minute confession, though. He did not move a muscle or change his expression.

The custom of the time held for the condemned to ride atop the coffin. But Boyington received permission to instead walk behind the horse-drawn cart that carried it. He was dressed in a black suit and a fine, silk hat and accompanied by Hamilton and Edward Olcott, one of his lawyers.

A huge crowd had turned out to watch the spectacle and although Boyington occasionally waved to an acquaintance standing at the edge of the sidewalk on Government Street, it mostly was not a sympathetic audience. Few doubted Boyington's guilt.

A foot troop known as the Home Guards and the City Troop on horseback, each with a brass band, escorted Boyington to the execution spot west of Palmetto Street at four o'clock. He saw the gallows, specially constructed for this day at a cost of sixty dollars, and the color drained from his face.

"If I can succeed in delaying the execution till the appointed hour is passed, will you demand me from the sheriff?" he asked Olcott.

"It cannot be done, sir, the officers will most assuredly do their duty," the lawyer responded.

Panic gripped Boyington as he stared at the gallows and looked around at the swelling mass of people. The execution had drawn voyeurs from as far as New Orleans and even slaves to watch Boyington's death.

He tried to stall, reading from a long manuscript he had drafted. "My dear friends, an innocent man will now address you. I tell you with an open

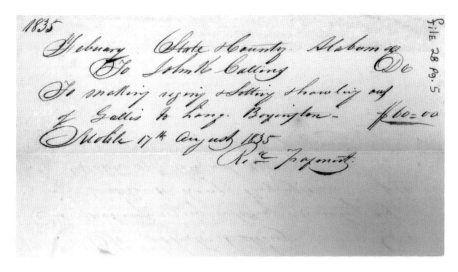

This bill for services shows that Mobile County paid sixty dollars in 1835 for the gallows used to execute Charles R.S. Boyington. *Mobile County Probate Court records.*

heart, that I am innocent of the crime I am accused of. I will not keep you long, but I must tell you that the pain I have been suffering is unjust. I am accused, yes, but I am the man being murdered today. Emotion makes my lips tremble as I address you."

As the speech dragged on, Sheriff Theophilus Lindsey Toulmin and his deputies became impatient. Finally, the sheriff had heard enough. He ordered Boyington, who had finished barely a third of his address, to stop. He motioned toward Hamilton.

"Mr. Boyington, the sheriff orders you to stop; the time is nearly expired. Ascend with me and calmly submit to the last necessary arrangement," the minister said.

"What, can't I read the rest?" Boyington asked.

"No, sir, not another page!" Toulmin said. "I am waiting for you."

Boyington turned to the surgeon who was to pronounce him dead and whispered, "Will it be possible to reanimate my body after I am executed?"

The surgeon shook his head, "I assure you it cannot be possible."

"What is the easiest way to die?"

"For the lungs to be moderately inflated," the doctor answered.

Boyington took off his coat and black tie. Sighing heavily, pale with swollen veins in his neck and temples, he raised his eyes to the heavens. Deputies placed a shroud on him and they walked up the scaffold.

Boyington's life was about to end.

Not even a year before, Charles R.S. Boyington's future seemed to hold so much promise. A Connecticut native, he had arrived by ship from New Haven in November 1833 with dreams of starting a new life in what then was one of America's most exciting cities.

A printer by trade, Boyington worked for a time for Pollard and Dade but found himself laid off in April 1834. Despite the setback in his professional life, his personal life was in good shape.

He was handsome, with a dark complexion and black hair. He had small eyes with large, heavy brows, and he walked with such an upright posture that he appeared taller than his five-foot-nine frame. At a ball held at the Alabama Hotel on Royal Street in December 1833, he met the love of his life, Rose de Fleur, the daughter of a French count who had fled his native country for Mobile. She would stick by him until the end, bringing him flowers and cakes during his incarceration.

Shortly after coming to Mobile, Boyington met Nathaniel Frost, who arrived from Connecticut the same year he did. The two had much in common. In addition to their shared New England heritage, Frost also was a journeyman printer. In Mobile, he worked part time for a newspaper while he tried to recover from tuberculosis.

The two men shared a room at the boardinghouse of Captain William George on Royal Street.

They became virtually inseparable. Boyington brought Frost meals and cared for him through his illness. In return, Frost—who came from a wealthy family—paid his unemployed friend's room and board and supplied him with spending money.

"What a whole-souled, generous-hearted young man Boyington must be," said George's wife.

On the afternoon of May 10, 1834, Boyington and Frost took a walk. Several people saw them near the Church Street Graveyard.

But Boyington was alone when he returned to the boardinghouse at about 3:30 p.m. Several of the boarders asked where Nathaniel was.

"Oh, he is somewhere; I am in a hurry, so I did not wait for him," Boyington said.

Boyington seemed restless, distracted and slightly pale.

"You went out walking, where is he?" one of the men asked.

"Yes, and I brought him back," Boyington answered.

Boyington walked to Morris and Fraser's Livery on St. Francis Street, which sported a sign reading, "Horses for General Hire, By Day, Week or Month, etc." Boyington paid for a horse and then made his way to the wharves, stopping at a general store to buy a pair of pistols, a dagger and some other items.

At eight o'clock, he boarded the *James Monroe*, a steamer headed up the Alabama River toward Montgomery.

The next day, passersby discovered Frost's body under a large chinquapin tree on the west side of Bayou Street, south of Government Street. Covered in wounds and blood, the body had five distinct gashes on the front that investigators determined had been made with a large dirk knife. Frost's head had bruises, and gashes covered his back, arms and legs, as well. Even in a lawless town that had grown accustomed to robberies and killings, the scene caused a sensation.

"The annals of crime have seldom been stained with a more diabolical act of atrocity than it is now our painful duty at this time to record," wrote the *Mobile Commercial Register and Patriot*.

"MURDER—$500 REWARD," blared the local newspaper the next day. Mayor John Stocking had offered $250 for the capture of Boyington, whom investigators already had fingered as the chief suspect, and another $250 if he was convicted.

Years after the affair, a Mobilian named J.J. Delchamps recalled sitting on the porch as a teenager with his friend James T. Shelton, who would grow up to become sheriff in 1859. Patsy, a twelve- or thirteen-year-old slave belonging to Shelton's father, came running up the street.

"Masa Jim, when I was looking for the cows a little while ago, I saw two men, a tall one and a short one, fighting under the big chinquapin back of a graveyard," she said. "They were hitting just so, making motions, the tall man fall down all bloody. I was scared and ran away."

Shelton asked Delchamps not to say anything; as a slave, Patsy's eyewitness account would be worthless in court, anyway. Later, Patsy would say that she recognized Boyington at the gallows as the short man she had seen during the fight.

—◆—

To investigators, Boyington seemed the obvious suspect. Witnesses had placed him with the victim on the day of the slaying. And Boyington's abrupt departure looked like flight. His reputation did not help. He was known to carouse in the less reputable parts of town near the riverfront, hanging around barrooms, brothels and gambling dens.

He was suspected of thefts in Boston and once was arrested in Savannah and tried on charges of horse stealing in Charleston. He was convicted of piracy there, as well, but won a pardon due to his youth.

Back at George's boardinghouse, the proprietor's wife found a neatly wrapped package of books and letters, with a note instructing her to give them to Rose de Fleur.

Having identified Boyington as the prime suspect in the grisly slaying and determined that he had fled town, it was now a race against the steamship for the lawmen. Officers Joseph Taylor and M. DuBois took off on horseback, catching up with the ship at Black's Bluff some 180 miles north of Mobile on May 15.

The officers found Boyington in the "ladies room" studying the hand of a man playing a card game called brag. Taylor placed a hand upon Boyington's shoulder. "You are my prisoner," he said.

"Why?" Boyington asked.

"You are charged with murder," the officer said, as a look of horror swept across Boyington's face.

The officers detained Boyington and found that he had a pair of pistols, a wallet, $95 and some silver coins. The large sum of money was suspicious for someone who had not worked in months and never had made more than $20 when he was working. Altogether, authorities estimated, Boyington had not cleared more than $100 during his entire time in Mobile.

Boyington maintained that he had won the money gambling but could not find the person he had bet.

During the return journey, Taylor began to harbor doubts about his prisoner's guilt and devised a test. He offered to let Boyington go if he left all of his belongings, figuring that an innocent man would not run. Boyington refused. The officer then proposed letting him escape with five dollars. Boyington again refused.

An immense crowd greeted the steamboat when it arrived in Mobile on May 16 with the shackled Boyington. The largely hostile crowd included slaves who were, in the words of a twentieth-century historian, "free for a day." Many in the crowd followed Boyington as he was taken to the city jail on Theatre Street.

"Kill him," shouted someone from the throng. "Throw him overboard," yelled another. "Hang him to the next lamppost—to the next tree."

The newspaper account was sensational.

"We have never witnessed such an excitement as was manifested on his arrival," the article stated. "An immense throng rushed to the wharves and the anxiety was intense to obtain a sight of the man charged with having imbued his hands in the blood of his friend."

Boyington made his first court appearance at ten the next morning for a preliminary hearing that lasted until six in the evening. A judge denied bail.

James Dellet, who would go on to serve in the U.S. House of Representatives, helped prosecute Charles R.S. Boyington. *Doy Leale McCall Rare Book and Manuscript Library.*

By November 16, the state was ready for trial. The prosecutor was Solicitor Berriman Brent Breedin, a short man with a neatly formed, square face. Later, he would find himself on the other side of the courtroom, prosecuted on charges of allowing criminals to escape. He was convicted, but a judge set it aside.

To help him try Boyington, Breedin brought in trial attorney James Dellet, who had served as the first speaker of the state House of Representatives after Alabama became a state in 1819 and later would go on to Congress.

Edward Olcott and Isaac H. Erwin represented Boyington.

The trial lasted until midnight on November 22. After an hour and a quarter, the jury returned with a unanimous guilty verdict. The next day, a Saturday, Judge Samuel Chapman sentenced the defendant "to be hung [*sic*] by the neck till dead on the twentieth of February, 1835."

With scarcely a dry eye in the courtroom, officers returned Boyington to jail, shackling and chaining his feet to the wall of his cell.

"Rarely have the feelings of the community been more deeply interested," the newspaper reported. "The murder was so cold blooded, so unprovoked, and so audacious, and the accused so self possessed, during the whole of the bloody affair, from the crime to the conviction, that wonder, and horror, were mingled with the ordinary feelings of curiosity and excitement on such occasions."

Boyington's last realistic hope was an appeal to the Alabama Supreme Court, which had been formed only recently. Prior to 1832, an assembly of circuit court judges considered appeals. That year, the legislature created the Supreme Court as a separate entity,

Boyington cited two main grounds for reversal: improper juror conduct and a defective indictment. A British citizen, George Davis Jr., had been allowed to serve on the grand jury that indicted him, and another juror, Chandler Waldo, had expressed an opinion about the defendant's guilt. In addition, the defendant argued, the indictment named the accused as Charles J.S. Boyington rather than his actual name, Charles R.S. Boyington.

The court heard the case on February 11, 1835. The court took the first claim most seriously but ended up affirming the conviction. The precedent set by the court did not last long. Two years later, a differently constituted high court, headed by future governor Henry W. Collier, overturned the rule on challenging grand juries.

But the reversal came too late to help Boyington.

Hamilton visited the condemned man in a desperate attempt to save his soul. The justice system had spoken, but if Boyington would make amends and repent, it was not too late to win reprieve from a higher authority.

While Boyington's brother was a minister, he had no use for religion, himself. But he welcomed Hamilton's visits as a respite from the solitude of jail.

"I am not offended that you speak so freely. I suppose you will not believe me, and I am sorry for it; but I have no confession to make," he told Hamilton. "I am not guilty of murder. I have my faults and I have been thoughtless and wild, but of murder I am not guilty."

Hamilton pressed Boyington, but he maintained his doubts about the existence of God.

"I cannot help it; and where I disbelieve, I am not mean enough to conceal it," he said in a cold voice.

Hamilton told Boyington that the days were counting down to the time when a noose would be placed around his neck. "In a few short moments after that, your breath will stop, your head will be still, your body dead!" he said. Hamilton urged Boyington to pray with him. Sobbing on his knees, Boyington looked up and said, "I will try, sir." But Boyington never gave in to the pressure.

"I have been a gay and wild youth. I have been guilty, but not guilty of murder—not guilty of the crime with which report has charged me," he wrote in a letter to Hamilton. "I swear it by the most solemn oaths that I consider binding."

In a long statement he had printed defending his innocence, he wrote: "I say that a person who should commit a murder under such circumstances might justly claim a discharge on a plea of idiocy or insanity."

Charles R.S. Boyington gasped for breath as he looked toward the sky. His court appeal had failed. His hope for a gubernatorial intervention had been dashed. The executioner placed a shroud on him; he ascended the scaffold of the gallows but refused to stand on the drop.

Reverend Hamilton prayed for Boyington's soul. "Give him strength to make his peace with thee and feel contrite deep down in his heart!"

Boyington grasped Hamilton's hand. "I thank you, sir, from the bottom of my heart."

The preacher asked Boyington for his last words. "Sir, I am innocent! I am innocent. But what can I do? When I am buried an oak tree with a hundred roots will grow out of my grave to prove my innocence!"

Boyington's body stiffened and tears rolled down his cheeks.

"I must make one more effort for my life—I must!"

Boyington leapt off the scaffold and tried to make a run for it. The crowd was aghast.

"Charge bayonets," the captain of the Home Guard shouted.

Weakened from his months of incarceration, Boyington did not get far. He fell to the ground, as soldiers quickly surrounded him. Daniel Geary, who was in the crowd that day, later recalled that not a single person offered Boyington any encouragement.

"The officers of justice immediately seized him—and then follows the scene that beggars description," he wrote.

Rose de Fleur had gone to the execution but ran away weeping as lawmen forced Boyington back up the steps. He struggled desperately, but weakly. His bound hands came loose, and he scratched the hangmen and tore at their clothes. The officers readjusted the noose and shoved him off the platform.

It was far from a clean execution.

Boyington somehow managed to get his hands between his neck and the rope. Officers pulled his hands apart. He writhed for half an hour before going limp.

The horrified crowd shrieked at the spectacle.

"Oh, it is like murder!" someone shouted. "It is murder."

The *Mobile Commercial Register and Patriot* was unmoved, however. "To the last he made no acknowledgement of his guilt," the paper reported the next day. "To say the least, however it is a matter of doubt if his harangue to the assembly did not excite prejudice against him, rather than sympathy in his behalf."

In the decades following the execution, doubt about the justice of it lingered.

After the trial, a man named John Casselle swore out an affidavit maintaining that he had seen Frost—alone—on Water Street at 3:00 p.m. or later on the day of the slaying. If true, that would have proven that Frost and Boyington had separated on Government Street during their walk.

In 1847, under the headline "Wrong Man Hung [*sic*]," the *Albany Evening Journal* reported the deathbed confession of the landlord in whose house the murder was committed. One key detail clearly was wrong: the slaying did not occur in a house. Did that make the story bogus, or was it merely a detail confused by time and distance?

J.C. Richardson, a lawyer in Hayneville, Alabama, referenced the Boyington case during his closing argument to a jury in 1894. In attempting to cast doubt on circumstantial evidence, he told jurors a woman named

Florence White, having sent for the Mobile police chief, reached underneath her pillow and retrieved a large, gold watch and chain, along with a diamond ring. She confessed that she and her man had followed Boyington and Nathaniel Frost. They waited for their opportunity and then stabbed Frost when he was alone.

The son of Mobile newspaper editor and author Erwin Craighead challenged that account, however, in a letter to the writer of a magazine article recounting the supposed White confession.

In the decades that followed the execution, according to lore, a great oak tree did rise from the spot where Charles R.S. Boyington was hanged. Boyington's body was buried sixty yards from where a great oak sits today.

Chapter 4

THE COPELAND CLAN AND THE BURNING OF MOBILE

As night fell over Mobile on October 7, 1839, a band of men decked out in fake whiskers, false mustaches and other disguises waited at the edge of the city. Some wore green eyepatches; others dressed like sailors. They came armed with false keys, lock picks and crowbars, along with revolvers, bowie knives and dark lanterns.

The men had planned for this night for weeks, casing the city's commercial district and making note of where the most valuable merchandise was. At nine o'clock, a half dozen friendly members of the city guard sent word that the coast was clear.

By ten o'clock, the men started out. They used a key to open a fancy dry goods store, swiping $15,000 worth of fine silks, muslins and other items. They pilfered silver watches and two to three gold timepieces, together worth $4,000 to $5,000. Some $3,000 worth of fine goods from a large clothing store disappeared into the burglars' hands.

At half past eleven o'clock—with a change of the city guard a half hour away—the burglars packed their loot into butcher carts they had procured, setting fire to the looted stores. As they made their way toward the waterfront, the bandits hit every store they came to. Wind from the southeast spread the flames, and soon someone yelled, "Fire!" and an alarm bell sounded on Conception Street.

The men worked through the rest of the night loading a pair of boats while chaos gripped the city. Just before daylight, two fully packed vessels shoved off toward Dog River, some ten miles south of Mobile, arriving at about 8:00 a.m.

Tired but satisfied, the thieves held a meeting to report their haul: an estimated $25,000 worth, including an abundant supply of liquors and groceries. They divided the score, with the three leaders—Gale H. Wages, Charles McGrath and James Copeland—taking about $6,000 worth. They each selected the finest and most expensive items for themselves, packing jewelry, silks and other goods into trunks.

The Wages and Copeland Clan had struck again.

Meanwhile, Mobile was in flames. The fire had come just five days after another conflagration at a furniture store on Dauphin Street burned a city block.

This one was far more devastating, and it hardly

OUR CLAN NOW COMMENCED OPERATIONS ANEW. WE SEIZED AND CARRIED OFF GOODS FROM ANY AND EVERY STORE WE CAME TO.

Among other crimes, James Copeland confessed to starting one of the most devastating fires in Mobile's history in 1839 as cover for looting stores throughout downtown. *Doy Leale McCall Rare Book and Manuscript Library.*

could have come at a worse time. The city was in the throes of one of its periodic yellow fever outbreaks, which meant that many able-bodied citizens were out of the city and many of the men who remained were sick.

The police and militia roused people from their homes so they could blow them up in a desperate attempt to create firebreaks to stop the flames from spreading.

Commission merchant Duke Goodman wrote to lawyer and politician James Dellet the next day that he had managed to save most of the furniture from his house, which had been destroyed.

The city awoke that day to find much of Dauphin Street, between Conception and Franklin Streets, in ashes. Some five hundred buildings had burned on several blocks to either side of Dauphin Street. Hundreds now were homeless. Investigators estimated the monetary loss at $2 million.

Sifting through fourteen demolished blocks, authorities fixed the blame on arson.

"Can it be possible there can be found in human shape, such base, fiendish monsters?" the *Mobile Mercantile Advertiser* asked its readers on October 9. "Mobile seems indeed a doomed city. Have we not drank [*sic*] deep enough of the bitter cup of adversity and affliction? When will our calamities end?"

It turns out, the calamities were not yet over. That very day, a third fire in seven days broke out, this time in an unoccupied room of the Mansion Hotel on the southeast corner of Conti and Royal Streets. The Planters and Merchants Bank and the nearly completed United States Hotel also burned.

A week later, Mobile still was a like a war zone, according to the *Mobile Commercial Register*.

"We walk among ruins, some of which threaten to topple down upon our heads," the paper reported on October 18.

The origins of the October 1839 fires never have been definitively pinned down. Copeland, in a confession first published in 1858, mentioned setting fires to cover his gang's looting. An 1843 newspaper article laid the blame on an escaped slave who supposedly had organized secret meetings with hundreds of other slaves. The conspirators, according to this account, mulled over the idea of murdering whites but then shifted to arson as part of a plot to gain freedom.

———•———

Layer after layer of legend and fact have piled on one another over the years to an extent that makes it impossible to separate the two when it comes to the Wages and Copeland Clan. The tales of depravity are so extensive and so voluminous that they seem impossible to represent the un-exaggerated truth—particularly considering the relative lack of attention the outlaws generated in the press during their own time.

Many of the details of their mid-nineteenth-century crime spree come from Copeland's own confession, given to the Mississippi sheriff who arrested him. Already a condemned man, Copeland at the time may have seen no downside to embellishing his own exploits.

What's more, the lawman himself had incentive to exaggerate. He paid to have the long confession printed in pamphlet form and peddled it throughout the Southeast, battling allegations for libel from three of Mobile's most prominent lawyers along the way.

Regardless of where the fact ended and the myth began, the Copeland name was enough to inspire shudders for decades along a wide swatch of the Coastal South. The name appears in many of the local county histories commissioned by the Works Progress Administration during the Great Depression in the 1930s.

A retired pension agent wrote a chapter on the gang in a book of his travels published in 1935. Parents in backwoods communities in Mississippi whispered the name of James Copeland to prod disobedient children to good behavior.

The story began on January 18, 1823, with the birth of a male child some ten miles from the Alabama line in the Pascagoula River Valley in rural Mississippi. That child was James Copeland, and his life of crime began twelve years later with the theft of a pocketknife from a neighbor.

Sent by his mother to Peter Helverson's farm to get some vegetables, the young Copeland asked Mrs. Helverson if he could borrow the knife. She agreed but asked that he be careful with the tool, since it had been a present. James promptly hid the knife and then lied that he had lost it. He pretended to search, eventually leaving the disappointed woman behind.

"I was all the time laughing in my sleeve, to know how completely I had swindled her," he later told the sheriff in his confession.

James claimed he bought the knife in Mobile. His mother, by his own account, upheld his "rascality."

From there, he was off. He helped his brother, Isham "Whin" Copeland, steal a cartload of the Helversons' finest pigs and haul them to Mobile, where they fetched two dollars a head. He swindled his classmates out of pocketknives and money. He would lie to get them flogged. All the while, his mother would run interference for him.

Copeland was still a boy when he faced his first serious legal trouble. Caught by Peter Helverson trying to steal from him again, Copeland found himself staring at criminal charges. That is when he met Wages, his future criminal partner. Wages, who was about six years older, discussed Copeland's options—including the possibility of killing witnesses.

In the end, they settled on arson. Before Copeland's trial arrived, the Jackson County Courthouse went up in flames. The conflagration destroyed the building, records and all.

Not long after that, Copeland formally joined Wages's gang, taking an oath on a Bible in a wigwam near Mobile where the clan made its hideout:

"You solemnly swear upon the Holy Evangelist of Almighty God, that you will never divulge, and always conceal and never reveal any of the signs or passwords of our order; that you will not invent any sign, token or device by which the secret mysteries of our order may be made known; that you will not in any way betray or cause to be betrayed any member of this order—the whole under pain of having your head severed from your body—so help you God."

He pledged to keep the clan's secrets and accepted signs and passwords. He learned the secret alphabet invented by John Murrell, a notorious outlaw from Tennessee, from which Wages supposedly had broken.

"We ranged that season from one place to the other, and sometimes in town, stealing any and everything we could," he said during his confession.

The plunder included beef, hogs, sheep and sometimes a fine horse or mule—"and occasionally a negro would disappear."

———•———

Back at the gang's hideout on October 8, 1839, Copeland, McGrath and Wages took three separate routes to Apalachicola, Florida. They sold most of their loot in a wealthy neighborhood near the Chattahoochee River. An older woman bought jewelry from Copeland, who feigned illness and wrangled an invitation to stay in her home.

Copeland sweet-talked the woman's seventeen-year-old slave girl and made arrangements for her to sneak away with him to be his wife. He told her that he would carry her to a free state.

The girl met Copeland, and the two stole a canoe and rowed for three days to Apalachicola. He stashed the girl, along with a slave that McGrath had kidnapped, in a swamp five miles from town. That night, Copeland and McGrath met some Spaniards at a coffeehouse and learned they had a schooner that they were going to sail to New Orleans.

The men made arrangements to smuggle their girls—along with a third escaped slave, taken by Wages—onto the vessel. The next night, they arrived at the Pontchartrain Railroad and headed into New Orleans. They ate breakfast at nine o'clock in the morning and then left on the *Bayou Sara* steamboat, eventually selling the slaves to a rich planter along the Mississippi River.

The seventeen-year-old girl who thought she was on her way to a new life in a free state with a charming husband fetched Copeland $1,000.

"My girl made a considerable fuss when I was about to leave, but I told her I would return in a month, and rather pacified her," he later told the sheriff. "I must here acknowledge that my conscience did that time feel mortified, after the girl had come with me, and I had lived with her as a wife, and she had such implicit confidence in me."

The three outlaws took their money and left for Mobile, stopping for a few days in New Orleans to rob a store. They landed in Pascagoula, Mississippi, and walked the remainder of the journey to Mobile. Each man had $4,500, which they hid in the ground, taking only $150 for expenses.

It was the beginning of a crime spree that would last more than a decade.

Wages, Copeland and McGrath set off for Texas in March 1841. Traveling up the Mississippi River, Copeland and Wages taught McGrath how to pray, sing and "give that long Methodist groan."

Within a few days, McGrath got a chance to try out his new Protestant act. At a Methodist Church in Natchitoches, Louisiana, he posed as Reverend McGrath from Charleston, South Carolina. He preached and then led the congregation in reciting an old hymn.

"Wages sang bass and I tenor, and we made that old church sound like distant thunder," Copeland later recalled.

McGrath preached some more, read Bible verses and sang another hymn. He left the church with some of his newfound brethren while Copeland and Wages found a gambling den.

The next day, McGrath returned to the church and told the congregation that he was poor. The parishioners took up a collection and gave him a fine black suit, a new saddle and saddlebags and fifty dollars cash. It was a ploy McGrath would repeat many times—preaching from the good book while his confederates stole horses from unsuspecting congregants.

Meeting outside Natchitoches, McGrath, Wages and Copeland made their next plan: McGrath was to rendezvous with the other two men on September 1 in San Antonio, Texas.

Wages and Copeland continued to a plantation, where they mixed poison and whiskey and killed the overseer. They stole ten slaves and two fine horses. Near San Antonio, they got $1,600 for the slaves.

The pair spent some time at a Mexican ranch in Texas, eventually luring a pair of ranch hands on the proposition of buying thirty horses and thirty mules. Executing a plan drawn up by Wages, Copeland pointed a gun at the sleeping younger man's head and waited for his friend and mentor to fire his weapon at the other man.

Wages fired, and Copeland almost simultaneously pulled his trigger. Both victims gave a suppressed, struggling scream and then died. Wages and Copeland spent the next day covering up their murders. They tied the bodies to a pole and then carried them to a sinkhole near camp, burying them along with their bloody clothes and hatchets. They then built fires on the camp where the bodies had been.

Then Wages and Copeland drove the herd to Wilkinson County, Mississippi, where they got $50 for each of the mules and an average of $75 for each of the horses. They sold them all except for four saddle horses. Two of those animals eventually fetched $100 each. Wages later got $150 for the horse belonging to one of the Mexicans and $25 for the one that Copeland had been riding.

The trip had netted $6,675. Wages and Copeland deposited the money in a New Orleans bank and spent the Fourth of July in the city.

The partners then took a steamship to Shreveport, Louisiana, and traveled by wagon to Texas. Along the way, they saw a slave driving horses. He told the men that his master beat him and did not feed him enough. Wages told the man he would take him to a free state. The slave stole three horses at Wages's request and joined him and Copeland.

They ran into John Harden, who had been stealing slaves in Tennessee. He told the slave who Wages had lured that he was an agent for an abolition society in Cincinnati. The slave followed Harden, traveling under the name John Newton, who promptly sold him along the Arkansas River for $1,250.

In February 1842, having reunited with McGrath, the bandits took a steamboat to Pittsburgh, landing on the Wabash River. They met an Irishman named O'Connor, a western trader with two large flatboats, and hired him.

Wages prepared a strong whiskey punch and left it to Copeland to deliver the fatal blow. He crept into O'Connor's cabin at sunrise and swung a lathing axe in the center of the sleeping man's forehead, a little above his eyes. The victim uttered a kind of suppressed shriek and was dead within minutes.

The three men went quickly to work, stripping the man's clothing and then tying a rope around the naked man's neck, tossing the cadaver overboard attached to heavy, cast-iron grates to weigh the body down.

"Oh God! When I look, it makes me shudder," Copeland would later say. "Even now it chills the blood in my veins."

They rubbed off the names of the vessels, *Non Such* and *Red Rover*, replacing them with the monikers *Tip* and *Tyler*. The boats, with cargo worth more than $5,000, glided down river. A man named Welter paid the men $4,500 and sent one of the boats down the Atchafalaya Bayou in south-central Louisiana and the other to his home along the Mississippi River.

Wages, meanwhile, returned from New Orleans with five barrels of whiskey and a load of gold coins. He placed the coins into three strong kegs made in Mobile so that each contained $10,000 worth. Wages, Copeland and McGrath covered the coins in clean, white sand and applied three coats of fresh paint to the containers. After the paint dried, the trio buried the kegs in a thick swamp along Hamilton's Creek near Mobile.

The men kept the remainder of the booty in cash, $625 each.

Upon returning to the wigwam, Copeland and Wages discovered that the clan had elected a new president. Reasserting control after a two-year absence, Wages announced that the organization's Vigilant Committee would make a report. Before that date arrived, he and Copeland formed a new group with a small number of men, including Copeland's brothers: Whin, Henry, John and Thomas. The new group then disposed of four "spies and traitors" from the original group; their bodies floated from the Mobile wharf down the river channel.

———•———

Two years later, in 1846, Wages married and built a house in Hancock County, Mississippi. He dug up the kegs of gold and reburied them in Catahoula Swamp about two miles from the homestead. He marked the new hiding place by a large pine tree and gave Copland a diagram to its location.

The following year, Copeland, his brother John, Allen Brown and McGrath hatched a plan to rob the house of a ferry operator named Eli Moffett, who had a contract to construct a bridge in Perry County, Mississippi. They decided to strike while Moffett was away from his home in the northern Mobile County community of Wilmer and planned to leave his family unharmed.

"That, I opposed, for I never believed in leaving any witnesses behind to tell what I had done," Copeland told Perry County sheriff James Robinson Soda Pitts during an extended confession.

The bandits stormed the house just after dark on December 15, 1847. When Moffett's wife, Matilda, refused to cooperate, John Copeland struck her head, and James Copeland delivered several blows of his own. They ransacked the home but found only a small amount of money before setting the house on fire.

COPELAND'S CONFESSION TO THE SHERIFF, DR. J. R. S. PITTS, WHILE IN PERRY COUNTY PRISON.

James Copeland gave an extended confession to Perry County (Mississippi) sheriff James Robinson Soda Pitts just before his execution in October 1857. *Doy Leale McCall Rare Book and Manuscript Library.*

They thought Matilda Moffett was dead, but she managed to survive the beating and fire.

The stage for the downfall of the Wages and Copeland Clan was set by a decision that Copeland fought—to enter the counterfeiting business. He believed it unwise but reluctantly agreed to join his compatriots.

Allen Brown got himself arrested on counterfeiting charges. Later, Wages and McGrath got into a heated argument with a regulator named James A. Harvey over a forty-dollar note. Brown had sold a farm to Harvey. When Harvey discovered that Brown did not have proper title to the property, he refused to pay. He ended up shooting and killing both Wages and McGrath.

Responding to a $1,000 reward offer from Wages's parents, James Copeland put together a revenge party armed with double-barrel shotguns, pistols and bowie knives. The men set off for Perry County, Mississippi, on July 8, 1848. They arrived the following Saturday in what is present-day Forrest County to find the Harvey home empty.

The men entered the house and made portholes on every side so they could fire upon Harvey as he approached. They took turns, in two- and three-hour shifts, watching for the homeowner's return. It was a monotonous affair. Copeland and his men ate figs, peaches and watermelon, destroying more than they consumed.

In the afternoon, hunger set in, and Copeland proposed going to Daniel Brown's house to get some meat and bread. But the others objected to the mile walk. Instead, Sam Stoughton gathered twenty ears of corn while Jackson Pool got a load of wood to make a fire.

"That is precisely what betrayed us—the smoke issuing from the chimney house," Copeland later recalled.

As night fell, John Copeland took his turn on watch. Stoughton, Pool and Copeland sat on the veranda, talking in muted voices. They saw a large, white fowl run through the yard, fifteen or twenty yards from them.

Pool took it as a warning.

"Boys, I shall be a dead man before tomorrow night!" he said. "That is an omen of my death!"

Stoughton laughed, telling him that if he were a dead man, he was quite a noisy corpse.

"I did wrong in making fire in the house," Pool insisted.

All of the men had difficulty sleeping. They discussed giving up but decided to wait to see if Harvey returned after breakfast. Between eight and nine o'clock the next morning, while the Copland gang was eating figs and peaches, John Copeland called out, "Boys, here comes a young army of Black Creek men!"

The men ran into the house. Pool grabbed his gun.

"Boys, take your guns," he yelled.

The approaching men separated, and someone said, "Come on, boys, here they are!"

Copeland ducked out of the house at first opportunity, darted around a large fig tree and gazed back at the house. Pool was standing in the door. Harvey came around the corner of the house to Pool's right and jumped into the veranda. Pool shot, striking Harvey's left side. Harvey returned fire, hitting Pool in the side.

Pool staggered into the yard, and another man shot him in the chest.

Stoughton and John Copeland jumped out of the door and ran. James Copeland turned as the crowd ran around the house. A gunshot whistled past Copeland's head. Hearing a barrage of gunfire, he ran so hard that, to him, he seemed to be flying above the ground. When he felt he no longer was in danger, he stopped and reflected on his life, vowing to become a Christian and renounce his criminal ways.

It was not until he was away from the gun battle that he realized he had lost the diagram to the treasure Wages had buried in the Catahoula Swamp.

Copeland later came across his brother, who was hiding in waist-deep mud, and learned that Stoughton also had made it out. Wages's father happily paid the second half of the reward, in part with livestock.

Harvey, meanwhile, lingered for ten days before succumbing to his mortal wounds on July 25.

Stoughton later got arrested trying to sell his reward oxen. He died in prison.

Copeland took to drinking.

In the spring of 1849, he found himself with three of his brothers at a grocery store near Dog River, about twelve miles from Mobile. Drunk and paranoid, Copeland tried to kill a man named Smith, who stabbed him in the collarbone in self-defense.

Copeland staggered out of the store and ran about two hundred yards before collapsing. His brothers carried him two miles. An arrest party, following the blood trail, came and took him into custody. He pleaded guilty to larceny in order to avoid a murder charge and served four years of hard labor in Wetumpka, Alabama.

The end of Copeland's sentence, though, was only the beginning of his legal problems. He would never see freedom again.

J.R.S. Pitts, the Perry County sheriff, was waiting to extradite Copeland back to Mississippi to stand trial for the murder of Harvey. The trial opened on September 16, 1857, and the jury convicted him a day later. Judge W.E. Hancock pronounced the death sentence on September 18.

The date of the execution, October 30, 1857, was a clear and beautiful day, with a bright blue sky. On the banks of the Leaf River, about a quarter mile from the county seat of Augusta, Mississippi, Copeland was hanged for his crime. As Sheriff Pitts put it, Copeland "expiated his bloodstained career on the scaffold."

The night before his execution, Copeland penned a letter blaming his mother's indulgence. "You are knowing to my being [*sic*] a bad man and dear mother, had you given me the proper advice when young, I would now perhaps be doing well," he wrote.

James Copeland was hanged on October 30, 1857, for the murder of James A. Harvey. *Doy Leale McCall Rare Book and Manuscript Library.*

Decades after Copeland's execution, the legend of the Copeland and Wages Clan has both grown and come under scrutiny. Treasure hunters for years have searched in vain for the buried gold. A Perry County man is said to have found the secret map but could not understand its markings. He showed it to people in Mobile; a prominent citizen supposedly asked to look at the document and then ran off with it.

According to legend, a black man named Wash Denton later dug up Copeland's body and carried it by horse to the home of J.B. Kennedy, who cut off the flesh and soaked the bones in vinegar. After they dried, Kennedy put the skeleton together with wire and buried the flesh at the old Denton place.

The skeleton ended up on display at a drugstore in Moss Point, Mississippi, along the Gulf coast. Another version of this tale names the establishment as McInnis and Dozier Drugstore in Hattiesburg. But at any rate, it has not been seen since the early 1900s.

Copeland's arrest on the larceny charge in 1849 brought one short mention in the *Alabama Planter* newspaper on April 1: "James Copeland, one of the gang of ruffians who have so long infested this country, was yesterday brought to the city, by a person named Smith."

Would a band whose exploits were as widespread and dastardly as legend later declared not have attracted more attention? As historian James Penick put it: "In 1849, Mobile seemed blithely unaware that a ten-year reign of terror had come to an end."

EXECUTION OF THE NOTED OUTLAW, JAMES COPELAND, AT AUGUSTA, MISSISSIPPI.

October 30, 1857, was a clear, beautiful day with a bright, cloudless sky as executioners led James Copeland to the gallows erected about a quarter mile from the banks of the Leaf River. *Doy Leale McCall Rare Book and Manuscript Library.*

Another historian expressed skepticism based on the language of the confession, itself. Were those really the articulate words of a backwoods thief with little formal education? Or did the sheriff, Pitts, embellish?

Pitts had motive to conjure the most riveting account possible. He had the confession printed in Mobile and worked hard to sell it. His efforts landed him in jail for a time, charged with libeling three prominent lawyers named by Copeland as members of his gang—Gibson Y. Overall, George A. Cleveland and Cleveland F. Moulton.

George Cleveland, Copeland told Pitts in his confession, "traveled then in considerable style, with two large leather trunks, and they were mostly packed with this spurious money."

A grand jury indicted Pitts in October 1858, and he went on trial in the Overall case in February 1859. Overall was able to show that he was a schoolboy in Columbus, Mississippi, during the relevant period. Pitts was convicted and sentenced to three months in jail. The other two cases were postponed for two decades, but Pitts had to return to Mobile once a year—even while he was serving in the Confederate army during the Civil War—or forfeit his bond.

There might not have been proof that Cleveland and Moulton were part of Copeland's gang, but there is a fair amount of historical evidence that they were not exactly clean, either. George Cleveland was indicted on an extortion charge in February 1859, the same month of Pitts's libel trial. He also faced charges of gambling and of using his office as justice of the peace to enrich himself.

Cleveland and his nephew, Moulton, were indicted on a charge of "assault to murder." They beat that charge, but a jury convicted Moulton of a lesser assault and battery charge; he paid a $1,000 fine. And he was indicted on an embezzlement charge.

Augustus Brooks, who often posted bond for Cleveland and Moulton, was fined for selling Negroes without a license.

Even the tale of Copeland's entry into the clan—the supposed arson of the Jackson County courthouse—has been called into question. Courthouse fires in those days were, in fact, fairly common occurrences. Half of Mississippi's eighty-two courthouses have burned, some more than once. And would a fire, even one that destroyed court records, really have stopped Copeland's prosecution? The farmer Helverson could have made a new complaint, and a grand jury could have re-indicted the defendant.

After his three-month stint in jail, Pitts went on to medical school in Mobile. He enjoyed a distinguished career as a physician, a county superintendent, a state legislator, a presidential elector and a postmaster in Waynesboro, Mississippi. But his name never reached the prominence of James Copeland—the myth he largely created.

Chapter 5

THE ENIGMA OF JOSIAH NOTT

In the middle part of the nineteenth century, Mobile had a true visionary, a man who possessed formal training and a curious, scientific mind that resulted in new and modified surgical instruments. His work on the longtime scourge of the South, yellow fever, planted the early seeds that one day would lead to its eradication in the United States. "The Barbific cause of Yellow Fever is not amendable to any of the laws of gases, vapor, emanations, etc., but has inherent power of propagation, independent of the motions of the atmosphere, and which accords in many respects with the peculiar habits and instincts of Insects," he wrote, rejecting commonly held beliefs of his day.

And nineteenth-century Mobile was home to a physician of the first order, a classically educated doctor who brought the profession's best attributes to bear. He was mindful of the Hippocratic oath—"Do no harm"—in treating a vast cross-section of Mobile, from the city's elite to its slaves: "I can honestly say, gentlemen, and it is the proudest boast of my life, that for the first ten years of my professional career, I never refused to see a human being, night or day, far or near, or in any weather, because he could not pay me."

The same period also produced one of the most viscous racists Alabama had ever seen, a man whose pedigree and status not only made him an important voice in the South but also gave him credibility in the North, as well. "Slavery is the normal condition of the Negro, the most advantageous to him, and the most ruinous, in the end, to a white nation," he wrote.

Meet Dr. Josiah C. Nott, Josiah C. Nott and Josiah C. Nott.

Dr. Josiah Nott was an enigma—ahead of his time in matters of medicine and science but a retrograde racist, even by the standards of his own time. *Doy Leale McCall Rare Book and Manuscript Library.*

Nott was all of those things, an enigma whose seemingly contradictory views owed as much to his times as to the particulars of his upbringing.

He traced his roots to the early colonial period. John Nott came to Connecticut in 1604. His grandson, Abraham, became a Congregational Church minister. Abraham's grandson, also named Abraham, headed south after graduating from Yale University in 1787, eventually settling in South Carolina, where he ran a successful law practice. He went on to become a judge, serving as president of the South Carolina Court of Appeals in 1824.

It was here that Josiah Clark Nott came into the world on March 31, 1804. Despite his family's New England roots, Nott was thoroughly southern. He attended Columbia Male Academy and then South Carolina College.

The college's president Thomas Cooper espoused a vigorous defense of the South's institution of slavery, states' rights and the rejection of the Bible as the source of scientific truth. All of those ideas had a great impact on young Nott, and he would carry them throughout his long and prolific career.

The events of the day also made their mark on Nott during his formative years, particularly a slave uprising led by Denmark Vesey in 1822. The plotted revolt shocked South Carolina's white population; more than thirty people hanged, and another thirty were banished.

When Nott graduated in 1824, he became one of five male members of his large family to pursue a career in medicine. He began a medical apprenticeship in Columbia, South Carolina, and then attended the College of Physicians and Surgeons in New York City. Amid internal strife at the school, Nott transferred to the prestigious University of Pennsylvania, where he completed his studies and paid forty dollars for his degree in March 1826.

Returning to the South Carolina capital in 1829 to start his own medical practice, Nott three years later married Sarah "Sally" Deas, the daughter of a prominent South Carolina family whose patriarch served eight years in the state legislature and was a high-profile supporter of the nullification movement.

Nott furthered his medical training in 1835 with a year of studies in Paris, at the time the mecca of advanced medicine.

Medicine of the early nineteenth century had not yet undergone the revolution of knowledge that would transform the profession. There still was much about the workings of the human body and disease that doctors did not know. But by the time Nott packed up his family and headed to Mobile in May 1836, following in his father-in-law's footsteps, he already was one of the best-educated, best-trained doctors in America.

———•———

Nott was hardly alone in his move west. Mobile in the 1830s was a boomtown, fueled by the incredible profitability of the cotton trade. Although Mobile County was not a major player in the crop's harvesting, as the only port in the state, a large share of the cotton that Alabama exported went through the city.

It made many families rich and attracted adventure-seekers from across the South. Its population nearly quadrupled from 1830 to 1840, rising from about 3,200 to 12,600.

Nott opened his medical practice near the customhouse on Royal Street and quickly gained a following.

"Mobile is essentially a money making place," Nott wrote to a former student in 1836. He estimated that he would earn $8,000 to $10,000 in the coming year.

In a February 1837 letter to a friend, he wrote, "I have made a very fair start in the professional way and shall do well I think."

Nott's high opinion of himself was matched by his contempt for most of the established physicians in town. To the former student, he wrote in June 1839 that the doctors were "making a mockery of fortunes by the intrepidity of ignorance."

By and large, life was good. His wife joined Christ Episcopal Church. He helped found the Mobile Medical Society to improve the professionalism of his chosen field, and he served on a three-man committee to draft a code of laws for the organization.

By 1840, he owned nine slaves; that number would grow to sixteen by 1850, and his real estate holdings totaled $15,000. That placed him just a notch below the city's wealthy elite—a group of only about twenty-five men, mostly merchants, who had real estate valued at more than $30,000 at the time.

As his practice continued to grow through the decade, he opened an infirmary for blacks, free and slave, on Royal Street near the slave market.

With his private practice booming, Nott turned his attention to the area of medical knowledge. Over the course of several decades, he was a prolific writer, contributing to medical journals. In 1838, for instance, he published in the *American Journal of the Medical Sciences* his suggestion for improving the design of a jointed splint for leg fractures. He wrote that he has used the device to successfully treat three or four patients, including a slave who had fallen through the trapdoor of a warehouse and suffered a double fracture.

By the 1840s, Nott's medical acumen had begun to generate attention outside Mobile. He invented a number of surgical procedures and improved others. He exhibited calm during crises.

He drew an admiring account by biographer Arthur William Anderson, who wrote in 1877 that Nott "performed so well, with dexterity, boldness, and astonishing self-reliance."

Nott tended to keep his extreme race views out of his medical observations and demonstrated a willingness to take risks for the cause of scientific knowledge. He began experimenting with hypnosis as a method of treating "nervous conditions." He wrote of success treating one woman's acute pain from an infected molar. In another case, he removed two bones to treat a tailbone condition that would come to be known as coccygodynia.

He gave a talk to the Franklin Society of Mobile in 1846—for twenty-five cents a head—on "The Phenomena of Mesmerism," or animal magnetism, despite ridicule from the medical community.

The reviews of Nott's work, however, mostly were exceedingly positive, both among contemporaries and those who wrote decades after his death. In the *Medical History of Mobile*, in 1847, for example, Dr. Paul H. Lewis gushed that Nott was "one of the most competent and careful pathologists in the South."

Nine years later, the *New Orleans Medical News and Hospital Gazette* wrote: "Southern surgery has not been awarded the position to which it is entitled, and it is simply because our surgeons are too sparing of their ink; we know of no one better calculated to place us aright than Dr. Nott, and we are sure that his silence is not because he loves surgery less, but that he loves other subjects more."

Dr. William Augustus Evans, who became Chicago's first public health commissioner in 1907, praised Nott's legacy decades after his death: "Dr. Nott deserves that his name shall live."

Willis Brewer, in his history of Alabama, wrote: "As a man he is highly esteemed by those who know him best, for he unites the sentiments and manners of a Southern gentleman with the acquirements of a savant."

Nott's sterling reputation was not without merit. In matters of medicine, he was an innovator. In 1855, he published an article in the *New Orleans Medical Journal* about a tool he had invented to remove infected tonsils. A year later, he published a medical journal article about using wire splints instead of thin patchboard to heel broken bones.

He offered practical advice to surgeons for treating gunshot and other bone injuries and how to respond to problems after the initial surgery. Other areas receiving attention from Nott included treatment of necrosis, or dead bone, and chronic osteitis, or inflammation.

Throughout his career, Nott expressed skepticism for "heroic treatment," preferring to let the body heal itself whenever possible. He wrote, for example, that doctors should allow nature to heal splinters still partly attached to muscles and tendons.

Toward the end of his career, after developing a specialty in gynecology, he sought a middle ground on uterine surgery, writing that the uterus had been cut too much and burnt too much.

He developed a method to stop hemorrhaging of the cervix after operation and came up with a modified speculum for uterine exams and that he claimed was easier to carry for house-to-house visits. He also commissioned a New York instrument manufacturer to build a uterine catheter of his own design.

Well into his sixties, as a relatively new resident of New York City and without a great deal of experience in his newly chosen specialty, Nott became president of the New York Obstetrics Society.

Again and again, Nott put people's medical needs above his personal biases. He treated hated Union troops stricken with yellow fever and drew praise for his work responding to a munitions depot explosion that destroyed several city blocks in Mobile and killed two hundred people just after the end of the Civil War.

On no medical topic did Nott gain greater attention, though, than the scourge of the southern states since Europeans first landed in the New

World: yellow fever. It was a horrible disease, marked by headaches, chills, back pain and rapid rise in body temperature. Vomiting and constipation followed and then, days later, organ collapse. The vomit turned yellow and then mixed with black fluids.

Dr. Josiah Nott (not pictured) was one of the founding members of the Can't-Get-Away Club, which helped care for the sick and others left behind during yellow fever outbreaks in Mobile. *Doy Leale McCall Rare Book and Manuscript Library.*

The disease was as perplexing as it was panic inspiring. It would tear through cities with a vengeance some seasons and be completely absent in others. Its patterns had no apparent rhyme or reason. The only defense was to abandon the city at the first sign of an epidemic. Residents who could afford to would flee to safer ground and stay away until medical authorities declared the epidemic over after the first frost.

Those who could not escape would hunker down in their homes. Nott always remained to care for the mass numbers of sick. He was a founding member of the Can't-Get-Away Club, a nineteenth-century Mobile organization that catered to the ill and others who remained trapped in the city.

Nott paid a heavy personal price. In September 1853, he watched four of his children die in succession from the disease. His brother-in-law James Deas also perished. Yellow fever claimed his nephew Charles Auzé in November of that year. Even in an era when the death of children was commonplace, it was an unusual toll for one family to bear.

Nott made important advances both in the treatment of yellow fever and its possible causes. Benjamin Rush, one of the founding fathers and America's most famous early physician, counseled a harsh regimen of treatment: three doses of mercurous chloride, an herbal purge every six hours and bloodletting. He also recommended cooling the patient and administering quinine, a white crystalline alkaloid used to treat malaria.

Nott, however, rejected that course of treatment. In 1843, he found success stopping vomiting with creosote, alcohol and a solution of ammonium acetate with a glass of water every two hours. In 1845, he published "On the Pathology of Yellow Fever" based on his observations of five epidemics that had struck Mobile during his career and sixteen autopsies performed by himself and others. He correctly figured that the hallmark black vomit was the result of blood mixing with stomach acid. He concluded that the disease was a "depressing morbid poison" that people received through the atmosphere but was not spread person to person.

"Beware of the Lancet," he cautioned in treating patients. "I would lay down a general rule that this is not a disease which demands active depletion, either by blood letting or purging."

In DeBow's Review in 1855, he wrote: "More good is effected by good nursing and constant attention to varying symptoms than by violent remedies."

In an 1848 paper, Nott also challenged the theory popularized by Rush and others that "miasmas" caused by decaying vegetable and animal matter caused the disease or that unclean air played a role. Nott instead pointed to "reasons for supposing its specific cause to exist in some form of Insect Life."

Dr. Josiah Nott was one of the most successful physicians in Mobile and known throughout the nation for his theories on racial origins. *Doy Leale McCall Rare Book and Manuscript Library.*

He wrote of a "perfect analogy between the habits of certain insects and Yellow Fever" and compared it to cotton pests. He observed that weather patterns had no effect on the spread of the disease except that very heavy rains seemed to impede marsh insects and that frost killed them.

"Chaillé, I'm damned if I don't believe it's bugs," he said to a New Orleans colleague during an autopsy. Nott speculated that science one day would be able to identify "animalcules," using the Latin term for microscopic organisms that caused the disease. He wrote that there was "every reason to believe that countless species still exist, too small to be reached by our most powerful microscopes."

In another paper, he wrote: "Even animalculae, so infinitely small to our senses, many in turn become gigantic, compared to others yet to be discovered with more perfect instruments."

Nott clearly was on the right track and often has been credited as an early forerunner of the men who eventually would unlock the secrets to eradicating the deadly disease from North America. One of those men was William Crawford Gorgas, whom Nott delivered in 1854. He was part of the yellow fever commission in Cuba that proved that mosquitos transmitted the disease and ordered the draining of ponds and swamps, along with other protocols for halting the disease.

Some modern historians argue that Nott gets more credit than he actually deserves. Despite his references to insects, they contend, he was far from making the crucial link between yellow fever and mosquitos. Harvard University professor Eli Chernin in 1983 wrote that Nott's views were "often vague, muddied or inconclusive."

Still, without the benefit of a more advanced understanding of the nature of germs that medical science simply had not yet uncovered, Nott discounted the dominant thinking that actually made yellow fever worse for its patients.

—•—

As careful and open to new evidence as Nott was in matters regarding medicine, he exhibited a reflexivity toward race that was a hallmark of the nineteenth-century slave owner.

Although Nott treated black patients throughout his career, his writings reveal the cold and clinical way in which he viewed them. He warned in 1847 that it would be unsafe for insurance companies to write polices on human property on the plantations in the country. He feared that many fraudulent policies would be purchased for "unsound" slaves.

"As long as the negro is sound, and worth more than the amount insured, self-interest will prompt the owner to preserve the life of the slave; but if the slave become unsound and there is little prospect of perfect recovery, the underwriters cannot expect fair play—the insurance money is worth more than the slave, and the latter is regarded in the light of a superannuated horse."

And then? "That 'Almighty Dollar' would soon silence the soft, small voice of humanity," he wrote.

Nott's career as a physician firmly established in the 1840s, he began writing on ethnology, the study of racial and cultural differences. It was here that Nott achieved his widest level of acclaim. His many books, pamphlets and journal articles on the subject all revolved around the central premise of the inferiority of blacks—and, indeed, all other nonwhite races.

He dismissed any evidence of great, nonwhite civilizations. The ancient ruins of the Central American Indians proved nothing other than a talent for architecture. But Nott argued in a lecture delivered at Louisiana State University that too much emphasis has been placed on those architectural accomplishments, which he compared to the talents of beavers in constructing dams or bees of making hives.

Nott found those ancient societies wanting in the areas of art, culture, government and laws.

"Everything proves that they were miserable imbeciles, very far below the Chinese of the present day in every particular," he said.

White superiority was hardly a controversial idea in nineteenth-century America, particularly in the South. But Nott raised the argument to a new level, arguing that Negroes were not merely inferior to whites but, in fact, a separate and distinct species altogether.

While Nott's racist ravings had few dissenters in the Mobile of his time, the same was not true for religious heresy. His theory that blacks and whites were separate species required a rejection of the orthodox belief in God's creation of the human race in the Garden of Eden. Nott chose to confront this contradiction with a full-bore attack on the Bible.

"How could the author of Genesis know anything of the true history of the creation, or of the races of men, when his knowledge of the physical world was so extremely limited?" he asked in a lecture delivered at Louisiana State University in 1848.

Nott expanded on that in an appendix he wrote for *The Moral and Intellectual Diversity of Races* in 1856.

"The Bible should not be regarded as a text-book of natural history. On the contrary, it must be admitted that none of the writers of the Old or New Testament give the slightest evidence of knowledge in any department of science beyond that of their profane contemporaries."

Nott wrote of the different characteristics of various species of felines, elephants, bears and other animals. When white Europeans are placed alongside black Africans, he wrote, "they are marked by stronger differences than are the species of the genera above named."

Nott's forceful and highly public argument drew fierce reaction from church leaders who could not reconcile the doctor's views of multiple creations with the supposedly infallible Bible. Nott had harbored antireligious views at least as early as his college days, when he watched his mentor, Thomas Cooper, take heat for similar ideas. As his stature grew, he accepted—and at time appeared even to relish—conflict with the church.

Nott presented the veneer of scientific inquiry on matters of race, and his credentials lent his writings a cache that other defenders of slavery lacked. But his writings on ethnology lacked the careful attention to the scientific method of his published work on medicine. In "The Mulatto Hybrid" in the *American Journal of Medical Sciences* in 1843, for instance, Nott asserted—with scant evidence—that mixed-race people were less fertile than either whites or blacks.

He based his assertion on fifteen years of observation during his medical practice. Mulattoes, he wrote, were less capable of endurance, shorter-lived, more susceptible to female diseases and "bad breeders" more prone to miscarriages. Nott offered no statistics, though, and casually acknowledged that there were exceptions to the "truths" he had laid out.

The evidence Nott used to support his ethnological writings was comical at times. He wrote in *The Moral and Intellectual Diversity of the Races* that he had contacted three Mobile hat dealers and a New Jersey manufacturer to determine the brain sizes of various races.

At other times, he offered no evidence at all. He asserted that the Negro brain was smaller, with larger nerves and a different-shaped head, all of which proved that "the intellectual powers [were] comparatively defective."

He contrasted the white woman, "with her rose and lily skin, Venus form and well chiseled features" with "the African wench, with her black and odorous skin, woolly head and animal features."

The differences between the two were as great as that of a swan and a goose, or a horse and an ass, he wrote.

Nott attained his greatest fame with the 1854 publication of *Types of Mankind*, a bestseller that printed its tenth edition in 1871. Filled with crude racial stereotypes, the book expanded Nott and coauthor George Gliddon's ideas of multiple creations. At the top of the hierarchy was unquestionably the white man, specifically the white man of northern European descent. Nott considered Germans to be the "parent stock" of the highest modern civilization.

"Nations and races, like individuals, have each an especial destiny: some are born to rule, and others are to be ruled," Nott wrote in his portion of the book. "And such has ever been the history of mankind. No two distinctly-marked [*sic*] races can dwell together on equal terms. Some races, moreover, appear destined to live and prosper for a time, until the destroying race comes, which is to exterminate and supplant them."

Nott maintained that the characteristics of the separate races had not changed in thousands of years, observable from the writings and drawings of ancient Egyptians, no matter what climate members of those races lived in.

"Numerous attempts have been made to establish the intellectual equality of the dark races with the white; and the history of the past has been ransacked for examples; but they are nowhere to be found. Can any one call [*sic*] the name of a full-blooded Negro who has ever written a page worthy of being remembered?"

It flowed naturally from such thinking that the enslavement of an entire race of people was justified; in fact, it was beneficial to the enslaved.

"Slavery is the normal condition of the Negro, the most advantageous to him, and the most ruinous, in the end, to a white nation," Nott wrote.

Blacks could achieve in certain areas, under certain limitation, Nott wrote elsewhere in the book. "Every Negro is gifted with an ear for music; some are excellent musicians; all *imitate* well in most things; but with every opportunity for culture, our Southern Negroes remain as incapable, in drawing, as the lowest quadrumana."

It was an argument Nott had made before. In his *Two Lectures on the Connection Between the Biblical and Physical History of Man*, Nott had argued that black Africans could make modest improvements under the care of white men but that those improvements maxed out after the second generation.

"Their highest civilization is attained in the state of slavery, and when left to themselves, after a certain advance, as in St. Domingo, a retrograde movement is inevitable."

It is but one of many, many writings in which Nott sought to justify slavery.

He did more than write to defend the institution. He acted, as well. In August 1856, he served on a "vigilance committee" that condemned a pair of booksellers, William Strickland and Edwin Upson, for selling "incendiary" titles like *Uncle Tom's Cabin* and the works of black freedom fighter Frederick Douglass. Citizens painted over signs, and the committee delivered an ultimatum for the businessmen to leave the city within five days.

Upson later recalled that Nott and two other physicians confronted him in a room at the Battle House Hotel. Dr. J.H. Woodcock had a carriage and rope and was prepared to hang him, according to Upson's account.

Strickland returned to Mobile in January 1858 to try to collect $25,000 in debts owed to his business. Instead, he was confronted by a $250 reward for anyone who would point out the "lurking place of William Strickland."

"It is the misfortune of Mobile that she has borne in her bosom a set of bad, reckless, unprincipled, and lawless men—a 'league' dreaded and feared by good people but against whom they are powerless," according to Strickland & Co.'s Almanac in 1859.

Upson, writing in 1884, also lambasted the vigilance committee. "It was such men as those composing the committee that ruled and finally ruined the South. Their inhuman outrages, perpetuated on good and loyal citizens, were the forerunners of the terrible war that soon followed, drenching the land in blood."

In the end, Nott lost nearly everything he had loved. After serving in the Civil War as medical director of Confederal General Hospital in Mobile—and living through the deaths of two more sons, one to battlefield wounds and one to typhoid—Nott returned to defeated Mobile a broken man.

Perhaps perceived as the greatest indignity by Nott was watching the Bureau of Refugees, Freedmen and Abandoned Lands turn his beloved medical college into a school for Negro children. Nott had lobbied the Alabama legislature for years to start the school and raised $25,000 from wealthy Mobile merchants to kick-start the effort. He made a trip to Europe to personally buy medical equipment and other supplies for the school, which opened in 1859 with a faculty of seven and three hundred students.

Its transformation after the war drew lusty cheers from *the Nationalist*, a pro-Union newspaper in Mobile. "Think of it!" the paper wrote.

Dr. Josiah Nott was enraged when the Freedman's Bureau turned his beloved Mobile Medical College into a school for newly freed black children. *Doy Leale McCall Rare Book and Manuscript Library.*

"A school of upwards of 500 children, who, this time last year, were chattels, now citizens of America, and already rivaling many of the most privileged children of our land in their knowledge of the branches of a common school curriculum."

It would be an understatement to say that Nott disagreed.

"I confess, it does not increase my love for the Government when I pass by every day or two and see two or three hundred negroes racing through it and tearing every thing to pieces—the chemical laboratory is occupied by negro cobblers," he wrote in an 1866 letter to a northern friend, Ephraim George Squier.

Nott wrote that he would "rather see the buildings burned down than have it used for colored children."

The previous December, Nott was even more blunt to Squier in his assessment of Mobile in the hands of Union troops and his continued belief that blacks were doomed to permanent inferiority: "God Almighty made the Nigger, and no dam'd Yankee on top of the earth can bleach him."

By January 1867, Nott had given up on his native South.

"I hope to leave the Negroland to You damd Yankees—It is not now fit for a gentleman," he wrote to Squier.

Nott did leave. He moved to Baltimore and then to New York City, where he lived for most of the rest of his life. He returned to Mobile after becoming sick with tuberculosis in 1873 and died on his sixty-ninth birthday on March 31. He was buried along with six of his children.

Chapter 6

RAISING (JOE) CAIN

In the winter of 1866, Mobile was a broken city. It had managed to escape the long Civil War without the physical pounding inflicted on so many other southern cities, but the economy was in tatters.

Prosperous and booming from a vibrant cotton trade on the eve of the conflict, the Union blockade and deprivation from the war had taken a heavy toll. The war interrupted virtually every aspect of civic life, including the city's famous love affair with frivolity.

Since the 1830s, social organizations had thrilled crowds on New Year's Eve with elaborate parades. With most young men fighting for the Confederate army and the rest of the city supporting the war effort, those parades had been suspended.

The year 1866 was, according to the book *Chasin' the Devil Round a Stump*, a "year of doom for [the] Southland."

Amidst this despondence, Joseph Stillwell Cain stepped forward to lift the city's spirits. With six Confederate War veterans, dressed in Confederate uniforms, Joe Cain appeared with a charcoal wagon marching through the streets to the delight of the people and the shock of occupying soldiers from the Union army.

Cain had spent the previous Fat Tuesday in New Orleans and watched with admiration as revelers celebrated Mardi Gras. He returned to Mobile determined to spread the tradition to his hometown.

Cain dressed in Chickasaw Indian clothing, a fur skirt and deerskins, and wore long Chickasaw-style hair under headdress. The tribe had been

Joe Cain dressed as a Chickasaw Indian, Chief Slacabamorinico, and marched through the streets of Mobile, reviving Mardi Gras after the Civil War. *Doy Leale McCall Rare Book and Manuscript Library.*

carefully chosen, as it never had been defeated in battle, the perfect symbol for embarrassing Union soldiers who still occupied the city. Cain called his character Chief Slacabamorinico, and the group made raucous music as it marched.

To a humiliated city, it was a subtle act of defiance in the face of occupiers. Cain, after all, could not wave a rebel flag in front of the troops. During the parade, many Mobilians invited them into their homes.

"It meant a whole people could still look up—look up in pride—and still keep going on," states *Chasin' the Devil.*

And that is how Mobile's modern Mardi Gras celebration started. Cain returned the following Fat Tuesday dressed in a tall, plumed hat and red knee boots with spurs. He and his band called themselves the Lost Cause Minstrels, and their parade drew a trail of delighted children.

By 1868, Cain was accompanied by sixteen Confederate veterans, including future judge Oliver Semmes, the son of Confederate admiral Raphael Semmes. The Order of Myths (OOM), Mobile's oldest current Mardi Gras organization, joined the celebration that year.

At least, that's the legend. That's the version every Mobilian, from native son to transplant, learns. It has been repeated in scores of books, newspapers and magazine articles over the decades.

But it almost certainly is not true.

Mobile author and folklorist Julian "Judy" Rayford persuaded Joe Cain's grandson to consent to exhuming the Mardi Gras legend's remains from a family plot in Bayou La Batre and reburying them in the historic Church Street Graveyard in downtown Mobile. *Doy Leale McCall Rare Book and Manuscript Library.*

Shoddy and inconsistent record keeping about a topic as frivolous as Mardi Gras, combined with Mobile's many fires, make it impossible to determine the accurate history of the city's most famous Carnival icon.

The real Joe Cain was a minor Mardi Gras figure before the 1962 publication of *Chasin' the Devil Round a Stump*. That work marked the zenith of author Julian Lee "Judy" Rayford's long effort to elevate Cain's stature. He based his story on an oral history culled from interviews with old Mobilians and Cain's surviving relatives.

He was given to hyperbole, suggesting that Cain "was a genuinely great man, the greatest man in the entire sweep of Mobile's history."

The historical evidence of the legend is remarkably scant, however. Newspaper accounts in 1866 on Ash Wednesday—the start of the Catholic Lenten period—contained no mention of Cain or mischievous merriment. The story was much the same in 1867.

It was not until 1868 that contemporaneous news accounts mention any sort of Fat Tuesday celebration. And it was the newly formed Order of Myths that received top billing. It noted Mobile's long tradition of elaborate New Year's Eve parades but stated that Fat Tuesday had been "unnoted" previously.

"The 'Order of Myths' have changed all this, and henceforth, no doubt, Mardi-Gras will be looked forward to with an anxiety as eager as that which attends upon New Year's Eve," reported the February 26, 1868 edition of the *Mobile Daily Register*.

The article reported that rain on Monday and Tuesday had made the dirt streets muddy and sloppy. Still, the paper stated, people enjoyed the parade and its theme, *Lalla Rookh*, based on the nineteenth-century Eastern romance by Thomas Moore.

The parade began on Royal Street at 8:30 p.m. It was preceded by the Lost Cause Minstrels, but the *Register*'s account made no mention of Cain or his alter ego, Chief Slacabamorinico.

"Early in the evening much curiosity and merriment was caused by the appearance of the Minstrel band of the L.C.'s—the society, itself, from, some cause or other, not turning out," the article states.

The paper's only reference to Cain was in an article describing a party held that night by the Washington Steam Fire Engine Company No. 8, of which he was a member. That gathering was hosted by J.B. Reilly, who had won a pair of horses in a fire company raffle.

"A large amount of champagne was quaffed, and the gentlemen present enjoyed themselves largely," the paper reported.

Among those listed in attendance was one Jos. Cain.

Pegging the start of Mobile's Mardi Gras celebration at 1866—or even 1867—just doesn't jibe with existing historical documentation, Cain's own recollections notwithstanding.

Mobile journalist Steve Joynt, who has extensively researched the city's Mardi Gras origins, uncovered convincing evidence that Cain was not even in Mobile on Mardi Gras Day 1867. He cites an article from the *New Orleans Times* on March 4 of that year listing visitors from Mobile expected to attend the annual parade commemorating the founding of New Orleans Fireman's Charitable Association.

The parade was held on the same date every year, and it happened to coincide with the day before Fat Tuesday in 1867. Cain himself wrote of staying for the Mardi Grad festivities the day following the fireman's parade and returning home determined to bring the tradition to Mobile.

"My experience on that occasion was so pleasant that I determined on my return home, that Mobile should have its own Mardi Gras celebration, and so it was announced in the *Mobile Daily Tribune* of that period," he wrote in a newspaper article printed near the end of his life (although he mistakenly indicated that the year was 1866).

Mardi Gras myth holds that Joe Cain and his fellow Confederate military veterans participated in the first Fat Tuesday celebration. The others who accompanied Cain may have been veterans, but Cain was not. Records on file at the Alabama Department of Archives and History show that he received an exemption from military service due to his vital role as clerk of the city's Southern Market.

At various points, Cain has been mentioned as the first Folly character to ride on the OOM emblem float and the inspiration for Dave Levi's decision to found the Comic Cowboys, a Mobile Mardi Gras satire group that has been skewering politicians and riffing the news every Fat Tuesday since 1884. Both claims also almost assuredly are untrue.

Mobilians jealously guard their status as the nation's Mardi Gras birthplace. The city traces those origins to shortly after its 1702 founding by French explorers. The Frenchmen had celebrated the holiday of their homeland at Fort Maurepas in what is now Ocean Springs, Mississippi. The settlers did not mark the season in 1702 because they were so busy transferring the colonial capital from Fort Maurepas to the Mobile River. But celebrations returned the following year with a few people donning masks and painting their faces red.

The Société de la Saint Louis formed in 1704 in the city's previous location on the Twenty Seven Mile Bluff. Dancing, eating and excessive drinking had become part of the festivities by 1705.

In 1711, a French soldier named Nicolas L'Anglois founded the Boeuf Gras Society, which celebrated Shrove Tuesday, or the day before Lent. The Carnival society celebrated with a giant bull's head pushed on wheels on Royal and Dauphin Streets. Eventually, the bull's head was replaced by a papier-mâché version imported from France.

The frolic would conclude with a ball and banquet at one of the city's finer hotels.

Modern celebrations in Mobile, with intricate floats, trace to the 1830s; like Joe Cain, their beginnings are an inseparable mix of fact and legend.

Michael Krafft, a young Bristol, Pennsylvania–born cotton broker, is said to have been dining with friends at La Tourette's restaurant on Conti and Water Streets on New Year's Eve in 1830—or, in some versions, 1831—when inspiration struck. After much food and drink, the group left and walked two blocks north and one block east until it reached a hardware store.

The store's name varies in different accounts. But it involves Krafft and the others grabbing rakes, hoes and cowbells from the outside the shop and then making a racket as they marched through the city, stopping to party inside various homes as they went.

"This coterie—partly in reply to an impertinence and more in sheer bravado—stole a splendid turkey hen from an old Creole restaurant keeper which had been fattening for a feast," journalist T.C. de Leon wrote in a 1911 account. "This they carried her and she never recognized it until they confessed."

The group ended up at the home of Mayor John Stocking Jr. at the corner of Government and Franklin Streets. From de Leon's version: "So jovial was the party under holiday hearths that they decided to serenade the Mayor."

Charles Kennerly, who purportedly was among the marchers that evening, provided this alternate account in 1870: "The participants were wholly unconscious of what an institution they were inaugurating."

The day after Christmas, Captain Joseph Post was aboard his ship on Government Street Wharf. Christmas day fell on a Sunday. He found Michael Krafft, who went to the Commerce and Conti Streets corner hardware store of Joseph Hall.

Krafft sat in the doorway and accidentally dislodged a rake, and a string of cowbells fell down on top of him. He gathered them and tied them to the teeth of the rake. Someone asked, "Hello, Mike—what society is this?"

"This? This is the Cowbellion de Rakin Society."

Commission merchant James Taylor joined, as did others. They found a half-starved mule and mounted it, riding him to a drinking house on Exchange Alley. They met up with "the boys" at the clothing store of E.R. Dickerson on Dauphin Street and made their dress, in the words of Kennerly, "as grotesque as possible."

Forty to fifty people formed a line at about 9:00 p.m. and ran into a messenger of Mayor Stocking, who invited them to his home. Eventually, the merrymakers moved on to the home of George Davis.

"But having partaken so largely of the Mayor's hospitality, we could do but little more than nibble at the viends and sip a little of his wine," Kennerly wrote.

Kennerly wrote that Krafft's frolic would have ended that year if it were not for Taylor, who led the New Year's activities. After Krafft died of yellow fever in 1839, one observer said, "Never until now have I seen a tombstone with a joke for an epitaph."

By then, the tradition Krafft helped start was fully entrenched. The Cowbellion de Rakin Society ran from 1831 to 1887, holding its last parade in 1880. The group's last banquet took place in 1912.

New Orleanians and Mobilians have argued for decades over which city has rightful claim to the nation's first Mardi Gras. Undoubtedly, New Orleans was the first city to stage elaborate parades on Fat Tuesday. But the concept of those elaborate parades came straight from Mobile's New Year's celebrations.

Samuel Manning Todd, a native of Utica, New York, came to Mobile in the 1830s and served as city treasurer and comptroller. He was active in the Cowbellions and exported that tradition to New Orleans in 1854. Brothers Joseph and William P. Ellison spent time in Mobile before moving to New Orleans. Joe Ellison held meetings for the "formation of an association similar to the Cowbellions of Mobile."

So Mobile invented the parades with floats, New Orleans moved the concept to the pre-Lenten Carnival season and Mobile followed suit. It is a circular relationship that binds both cities.

———•———

Nowhere but Mobile, though, has Joe Cain.

He was born on October 10, 1832, on the north side of Dauphin Street between Warren and Cedar Streets. He lived on Spring Hill Avenue in a neighborhood that once was home to the old Central Market. His parents, Irish immigrants, were Quakers from Philadelphia.

Parents Joseph and Julia Ann Cain came to Alabama by wagon in about 1825. Son Joe Cain worked as a cotton broker and held a number of public positions over the years, including coroner, the city's inspector of naval stores and clerk of the Southern Market. He fell in love with Elizabeth Rabby when he already was engaged to another woman. Before he could pursue Elizabeth, he first needed to perform the unpleasant task of breaking off his first engagement. In true Joe Cain fashion, here is how he pulled it off.

Pretending to be drunk, he staggered around during a fashionable ball. His mortified fiancée broke off the engagement herself. And her parents told him never to "darken our door again."

He married Elizabeth in 1855 and had five children and seventeen grandchildren.

Cain could be stern. His grandson Benny Thomas told Rayford about the time he got caught skinny-dipping at a mill at the foot of Eslava Street. The judge agreed to waive the fine if the boy's family would whip him. Joe Cain, by then an older man, walked the four blocks to the jail to retrieve his grandson.

"Boy, he hit me with that belt of his all the way home," he said.

Another time, Benny lied when Cain confronted him about a cherry he had taken from a tree in the backyard. Cain beat him with a barrel stove.

Cain's love of a good party is not in dispute, however. He was barely a teenager when he helped found the Tea Drinkers Society in 1846. They called themselves "The Determined Set," or TDS. The Tea Drinkers name comes from the group's slogan that they "never drank anything as weak as tea."

The group participated in Mobile's New Year's Eve festivities. Its last parade was in 1883. During the organization's golden anniversary, the organization paid tribute to Cain with a golden walking stick and a fine beaver hat. He was the group's last surviving founder.

Whatever the truth was about the date Cain first donned his Indian costume, the legend was in full swing by the middle of the next decade. An 1874 newspaper features a drawing of a lunatic with upraised arms holding large drumsticks over a drum labeled "L.C. Minstrel Band." It invites revelers to celebrate with Chief Slacabamorinico, who would journey from Wragg Swamp: "Old Slac and his boys—and heavy dogs they are!—emerge from the ground between one and 2:00 p.m. on Mardi Gras...This year, Old Slac invites all maskers, horse, wagon, foot, and dragons to join him in one grand procession through the city, the route and hour will be given at the proper time."

Cain's reputation survived his death. As grandson Benny told Rayford, "Every time Mardi Gras came, after he died, folks'd say, 'He ain't here, but he'd sure enjoy it if he was here.'"

Cain moved to Bayou La Batre, south of Mobile, to live with one of his sons in 1885 but remained clerk of the Southern Market until 1900. He died four years later at the age of seventy-two. An obituary in the *Mobile Item* called him "'the father' of Mobile's Myths."

Despite the fame in his own time, Cain's name seemed destined to fade into history before Julian Rayford.

Mardi Gras in Mobile during the 1960s had declined in importance. Booths had been banned in Bienville Square, along with mule-drawn floats and Cracker Jacks. Rayford believed the spontaneity had been drained from the holiday. He dreamed of a conversation with Joe Cain on a bench in the city park.

"I just wanted to make people laugh, they were so sad after the war," Cain told Rayford in the dream.

Rayford made it his life's work to raise Cain's profile. He wore down Cain's grandson Vance for years until finally convincing him to sign the papers allowing for Cain's body to be exhumed and buried in Mobile's Church Street Graveyard on February 6, 1967. The Excelsior Band, a Mobile Mardi Gras fixture since the nineteenth century, played "When the Saints Go Marching In."

The real Joe Cain held a variety of public positions, including clerk of the Southern Market. He was a volunteer firefighter and a renowned partier. *Doy Leale McCall Rare Book and Manuscript Library.*

Master of Ceremonies Martin Johnson said, "I commend his soul to the Maker, who most dearly loves such bright spirits as Joe Cain, father of modern Mardi Gras in our old city."

After it came to light that the family plot was in another spot of the cemetery, Cain's body was dug up a second time.

Rayford himself was buried next to Cain after his own death in 1980.

Chapter 7

"Pig Iron" Kelley, Gustavus Horton and the Wickedness of Mobile During Reconstruction

*J*ohn A. Brady was sitting at a table on the speaker's stand, furiously taking notes of the firebrand abolitionist William D. "Pig Iron" Kelley's address in Mobile under a bright moon when he became distracted by the sound of horses stomping on the bridge crossing the north side of Government Street.

Brady, a reporter covering the speech for the *Mobile Daily Times*, looked up thinking a horse was running away. He saw forty to fifty people running toward St. Emanuel Street. Most of them held clubs or canes raised in the air.

Brady did not think much of the scene and had returned to his note taking when he saw a perpendicular flash from a dense part of the massive crowd arrayed in front of Kelley. Brady jotted "shot" in parentheses in his notes.

The reporter remained unalarmed, however. He recalled a meeting he once covered in which a thousand shots had been fired into the air and regarded gunfire in front of Kelley to be a similar sort of firework accompaniment to the fiery speech. He interpreted shots number two and three in the same manner.

But then Kelley abruptly stopped talking, and when Brady jerked his head up, the speaker was gone. Most of the dignitaries who were on the platform were gone also. Others had dived to the floor. Only a few were still standing.

Still, Brady believed there was no reason for panic; he thought Kelley and the others had overreacted.

Then all hell broke loose. Brady heard a barrage of gunshots. He was on his way down the steps of the speaker's platform when he heard a shot

Pennsylvania congressman William D. "Pig Iron" Kelley's fiery speech in Mobile in May 1867 touched off a riot that led to two deaths and helped prompt a crackdown by the occupying Union army. *Doy Leale McCall Rare Book and Manuscript Library.*

whistle over the empty stand and strike the front wall of the old courthouse, which organizers had chosen as the backdrop for Kelley's historic speech. By the time Brady reached the formerly packed sidewalk, it was empty. Men were running in every direction.

Walking to the corner of Government and Royal Streets, Brady saw a large crowd of black folks in front of the stand. Two smaller crowds of black men gathered around what he figured were injured men. The alarm bell rang for the first time.

Brady ducked into a building on the southeast corner of Government and Royal Streets and took refuge with a number of white men. When the shooting appeared to be over, he made his way up Royal Street and ran into John Forsyth, a city alderman and publisher of the rival *Mobile Daily Advertiser and Register*, who was returning from a concert with his wife. Brady advised Forsyth not to go home, which was near the scene. Forsyth took the advice and escorted his wife back to Old Fellows' Hall, where the concert had taken place and which was the nearest place of refuge.

On the stage on that evening of May 14, 1867, was Gustavus Horton, one of the few prominent white men in Mobile who had remained loyal to the Union during the Civil War. Horton spoke of his "honor and privilege" to introduce Kelley to a crowd of some four thousand mostly black residents.

Kelley was a U.S. representative from Pennsylvania and a leader of the "Radical Republicans" who sought to impose harsher punishment on the defeated Confederates and take more aggressive action in lifting up the formerly enslaved population. His "Pig Iron" nickname had come from his longtime support for high tariffs on imports of his state's two chief manufactured products.

Kelley's stop in Mobile was part of a swing through the South to recruit new members to the Republican Party.

Kelley railed against the Confederacy and told the crowd that slavery was the backbone of that discredited cause. He said a disruption of freedom of speech and of the press contributed to causing the costly war.

His remarks were wildly popular among the large throng of black citizens before him. But they did not go over nearly as well with the smaller number of whites, some of whom began to heckle him. "Take him down," some shouted. "Put him down," said others. "Rotten egg him," said another.

Among the one hundred people on the stand with Kelley were occupying soldiers who were enforcing the restrictions of Reconstruction. Their presence emboldened Kelley in the face of heckling.

"Fellow citizens," Kelley shot back, "I wish it understood that I have the Fifteenth United States Infantry at my back; and if they are not enough to protect a citizen in the right of free speech, the United States Army can do it."

Kelley exaggerated. Behind him that night actually was the Fifteenth United States Infantry Band.

From Horton's perspective, the first shot from a pistol came after police chief Stephen Charpentier tried to arrest one of a group of hecklers, David Files. A horse or a horse with a wagon got loose, sparking panic. Four or five seconds after the first shots, several more rang through the air.

"The bullet that passed over his shoulder, came near being fatal to me," Horton wrote years later in a letter to a friend.

The mêlée left two men dead—a black man named Samuel Britton and a white man named Gabriel Olsen. At least ten more suffered injuries. Only one arrest was made.

The incident left a sour taste in Kelley's mouth that he would carry for the rest of his life. Years later, he told the Associated Press, "I once was shot and once had more than 60 shots fired at me. The latter happened, you know, in what was known as the Kelley riot in Mobile, Ala., in 1867, under Andy Johnson. While speaking there I was attacked by a very bad lot of carpetbaggers, marshalled and led by a cutthroat whose home is now well known in connection with a patent car. He meant to kill me."

The reaction to the riot was swift.

Major George Tracy of the Bureau of Refugees, Freedmen and Abandoned Lands was unambiguous about whom to blame when he made his report to Brigadier General Wager T. Swayne, assistant commissioner of the Freedmen's Bureau in Alabama. "The riot was undoubtedly commenced by whites," he wrote.

Swayne stated in his report to a superior that the disturbance did not appear deliberately planned, "unless possibly by a small party of ruffians." But he wrote that the police response was at best timid and inefficient.

"At the same time, freedom of speech and public orders have been greatly outraged in that city, by an element which is active in the spirit of rebellion, and presumes upon the sympathy of the police in this regard," he wrote.

Swayne banned outside assemblies, ordered guards placed at the fire companies and recommended that loyal citizens be put in charge of the civilian government. On May 22, General John Pope, the Third Military District commander, ordered the mayor and police chief removed from office and dismissed the aldermen and Common Council. Former Union army officer C.A.R. Dimon became police chief, replacing Charpentier, and reported to O.L. Shepherd, commanding officer of the Fifteenth Infantry.

Two months into a more aggressive military Reconstruction imposed by Congress, whatever hope Mobile might have had at a lighter hand had been extinguished.

The tensions that flared on that bright evening in May 1867 had been building for months, for years really.

Mobile escaped the physical devastation visited on many southern cities during the Civil War. The only significant destruction occurred after war's end when an ordinance depot on Beauregard Street burst into flames on May 25, 1865. The explosion killed some three hundred people and burned eight city blocks. Two ships sank in the nearby Mobile River.

Although Mobile had escaped bombardment during the war, its economy had suffered greatly. The Union blockade deprived its citizens of basic goods. Frustration reached a tipping point on September 4, 1863, when dozens of people—mostly women—marched from the community of Spring Hill into the city with knives and hatchets. They carried signs reading, "Bread or Blood" and "Bread and Peace" while they smashed store windows and looted businesses.

After soldiers refused to fire on the mob, Mayor Robert H. Slough persuaded rioters to disband on the promise of improving rations.

When the Confederate army's last resistance crumbled along the banks of Mobile Bay's eastern shore on April 9, 1865—the same day Robert E.

The only significant physical damage to Mobile from the Civil War occurred after the conflict had formally ended. A depot packed with armaments exploded on May 25, 1865, destroying eight city blocks. *Doy Leale McCall Rare Book and Manuscript Library.*

This illustration depicts the famous Mobile bread riot near the end of the Civil War, when angry citizens—mostly women—took to the streets to protest meager food rations. *Doy Leale McCall Rare Book and Manuscript Library.*

Lee surrendered at Appomattox Court House—Slough ordered a white flag flown.

The Union army marched into the city uncontested. Military commanders left only a small contingent in the city and chose accommodation with the local civilian government. It fit with the philosophy of Andrew Johnson, who became president after John Wilkes Booth assassinated Abraham Lincoln. The new president favored working with local government leaders. Courts resumed a month after the city's surrender.

Life in Mobile more or less returned to normal, albeit with a large black population now freed from slavery and a steady stream of former slaves flowing in from rural parts of the state. It was not a welcome development for most of the city's whites.

"Negroes free, negro schools, negroes everything, everywhere, anywhere, white men nowhere," wrote Mobilian Alfred Reynolds in a letter on May 12, 1865.

The notion that whites were getting shoved aside was a view widely shared throughout the South and even in places outside the Confederacy. That view lasted for years after the end of the war. An 1868 article in the *Omaha (Nebraska) Herald* spoke of Alabamians as "victims of the damnable and insufferable negro despotism."

"Fleeing from oppression unbearable, and from State crimes and tyrannies unparalleled in history, the people of the South, that people who once made it great and powerful, are escaping from the outrages of a barbarous rule and from their desolated homes, as men flee from famine and the pestilence," the paper reported.

Mobile's elected leaders in 1865 largely met the accommodation of their occupiers with resistance. Slough enforced the black curfew that had been in place since before the war, set high peace bonds for blacks accused of crimes in an attempt to force them to leave the city whether guilty or not and charged unemployed blacks with willful idleness. He refused orders from the military to release men from chain gangs.

Slough also routinely refused to accept the testimony of blacks during sessions of Mayor's Court, a practice throughout the South during slavery time but which had been ordered to end. In one case, the mayor dismissed charges against a white man charged with knocking over a "negro wench" and disallowed her testimony.

Some of Mobile's citizens outright refused to accept the Confederacy's defeat. One man was imprisoned for trying to transport large amounts of ammunition to guerrillas in the interior part of the state.

On June 17, 1865, the bishop of the Episcopal Church in Mobile refused Brigadier General Kilby Smith's request to include prayers for the president in his service.

The U.S. flag, Smith wrote late that year, was barely tolerated in the city.

"They are not welcome among the people in any classes of society. There is always a smothered hatred of the uniform and the flag. Nor is this confined to the military, but extends to all classes who, representing northern interests, seek advancement in trade, commerce, and the liberal professions, or who, coming from the North, propose to locate in the South."

Smith gave a negative assessment of the citizens of Mobile. He documented threats to destroy schoolhouses for Negro children and black churches, as well as assassination threats against black preachers.

"It is my opinion that with the exception of a small minority, the people of Mobile and southern Alabama are disloyal in their sentiments and hostile to what they call the United States, and that a great many of them are still inspired with a hope that at some future time the 'confederacy,' as they style it, will be restored to independence."

Captain W.A. Poillon, the assistant superintendent of the Freedmen's Bureau, wrote that civil authorities failed to accept the spirit of Swayne's order allowing black testimony in court. Poillon alleged injustice and wrote that the police department was "decidedly hostile to color," and engaged in a high number of false arrests.

"All hopes of equity and justice through the civil organization of this city is barred; prejudice and a vindictive hatred to color is universal here; it increases intensely, and the only capacity in which the negro will be tolerated is that of slave," he wrote.

Three of the city's newspapers kept up a steady drumbeat of sensational reports that kept the city's white population on edge. At one point, Major General Charles R. Woods, commander of the Department of Alabama, issued a warning to the *Mobile Daily News* for publishing baseless articles about impending Negro insurrections.

Harsh words morphed into violence on July 4. Slough denied a request by black residents to use Bienville Square in the city's heart for a Fourth of July celebration on the grounds that it would damage the park's lawn. But Smith overruled the mayor and described the six thousand people who attended as "well-dressed and orderly."

A violent confrontation ensued between whites—including the police—and blacks. Smith later would lay the blame on Slough and the police department.

"The enormities committed by these policemen were fearful. Within my own knowledge colored girls seized upon the streets had to take their choice between submitting to outrage on the part of the policemen or incarceration in the guard-house," he wrote.

Black residents fought back, demanding a "military mayor" and changes in the police department. Later that summer, Swayne persuaded Alabama's provisional governor to force Slough's resignation from office and replace him with John Forsyth, the newspaper editor and publisher. Slough was the only civilian official in Alabama against whom he had taken such action.

Forsyth had served as a minister to Mexico and a state representative, and had a short stint as mayor during the war.

Forsyth had run the Alabama campaign for Stephen A. Douglas during the 1860 presidential election and was with the candidate at the Battle House Hotel in Mobile on election night. His short stint as Mobile mayor after Slough's removal was marked by calmness and improving race relations even if Forsyth himself did not hold progressive views on the issue.

Jones M. Withers, a former Confederate general whose political rights had not yet been restored by President Johnson, replaced Forsyth after defeating Cleveland F. Moulton in a close and fraud-laden campaign in December 1865. The new mayor worked closely for a time with Swayne and even offered a $1,000 reward for information about the burning of a building owned by African Methodists that was rumored to be a new home for a black school.

But life for blacks in Mobile remained difficult, and relations with the white majority were tense. Black dockworkers went on strike in March 1867, demanding a raise from twenty-five cents an hour to fifty cents to match the pay of their counterparts in New Orleans.

That same month, Shepherd interpreted a funeral procession for a Confederate captain who had died in Tennessee during the war to be provocatively lavish and disrespectful and cracked down on the city fire companies.

The following month, a streetcar driver roughly ejected a black woman who had tried to sit inside the car; drivers regularly made blacks stand on the outside platforms. William W.D. Turner, an attorney for the Union League of Mobile, agreed to take the case to court, which further ratcheted up tensions.

On April 14, a black man named Roderick B. Thomas got on a streetcar that was waiting for the Sunday service at Government Street Presbyterian Church to end. Thomas refused the driver's order to get off the car, and following instructions from Mayor Withers, the driver unhitched the car from the horses. After a lengthy standoff, Thomas finally got off the streetcar and walked over to a group of freedmen.

When the church service broke up, the white congregants boarded and the driver re-hitched the horses. Thomas, who later would become a police officer and eventually Alabama's first black judge, tried to re-board, prompting a violent reaction with the white passengers. One man threatened to blow his brains out. Another man, Thomas Torrance, shoved him off the car. A fight between freedmen and a group of whites on the street followed.

A few nights later, someone fired shots after a meeting of the Union League, a political organization of blacks and sympathetic whites.

Around the same time, military authorities ordered the arrest of George M. Bonner, a justice of the peace who had sentenced a black man to be whipped in violation of the civil rights law. Bonner defended himself in a letter to the *Mobile Times* in which he said the former slave had failed to pay his fines and begged to be allowed to work off his debt.

"Now mark his conduct: He deserted my service several times; stole my horse from my stable several times and rode him the greater part of the night, and of length took every vestige of my clothing from my wardrobe," he wrote.

Then in May, white passions became inflamed after reports that black men robbed a white family along Dog River about twelve miles south of the city and raped the woman and her twelve-year-old daughter.

The toxic environment had been perfectly primed for an outburst by the time Kelley rose to address the large crowd on the evening of May 14, and his incendiary words were the match to the kindling.

At first glance, Gustavus Horton would have appeared an unlikely candidate to be a champion of black freedom. Although born in Boston, he eagerly insinuated himself into the Southern fabric of Mobile after moving there in 1832.

Taking a job as a cotton broker for a large mercantile firm, Horton owned at least two slaves and engaged in civic life. He won election in 1852 to the board of Alabama's first public school system, served as a church elder and as treasurer of the Samaritan Society.

His New England roots did not appear to bother his colleagues and neighbors in Mobile.

"He is a northern man with southern feelings, a first rate Loco of course, and a very respectable and intelligent Merchant," wrote Thaddeus Sanford in nominating Horton to the governor for the position of bank examiner.

The War Between the States changed everything, though. Horton opposed Alabama's secession and, unlike most others who had argued against the idea, refused to fall in line once war came. His position led to his professional and social ostracism, and it divided his own family. Two of his sons volunteered to fight for the Rebel army, and a son-in-law and fiancé of another daughter were Confederate officers.

Gustavus Horton, one of the few Mobilians to remain loyal to the Union during the Civil War, got his chance for redemption when military authorities installed him after ousting Mayor Jones M. Withers. Horton ended up getting convicted of violating the new civil rights law. *Mobile History Museum.*

"I have always been a Union man and opposed, so far as I could, all the secession movements that preceded the war and Rebellion," he wrote to a friend in 1879. "During the war I was one, of perhaps a dozen others in this City, who was openly known and recognized, as Loyal to the U.S. Government, and of course opposed to the so called Confederacy."

It was a costly stand. In addition to the social and business harm he suffered, he even spent some time locked up. The provost marshal ordered his arrest when he refused to sign a loyalty oath. Only his son-in-law's influence as a Confederate officer allowed Horton to avoid a longer incarceration; he signed the loyalty oath and returned home embittered after two days and nights in jail.

When the war finally ended, Horton hoped to benefit from his pro-Union loyalties. He was bitterly disappointed, however, at the conquering northern army's strategy of cooperation with the former Confederates.

"I am sorry to say that, the way things are now being managed, unless checked, will ere long place power and influence in the very hands that have been the cause of our troubles," Horton wrote to his wife almost three months after the war. "And if such should be the case, this will be no place for a Union man to live in."

Horton's prospects improved, however, after passage of the Reconstruction Acts in March 1867. He won appointment to a three-member board—consisting of two whites and one black—charged with supervising the registration of loyal voters.

After the Kelley riot, Horton got a chance for even more prominence. General Pope installed him as mayor and appointed former Union officer C.A.R. Dimon as police chief at the same time he swept out the aldermen

Harper's Weekly depicted the desperation of Alabamians receiving food rations in 1873. Nearly a decade after the end of the Civil War, the economy in Mobile and the rest of the South still was in shambles. *Doy Leale McCall Rare Book and Manuscript Library.*

and Common Council members, although military overseers quickly relented and reappointed two aldermen and five council members following a protest.

The *Nationalist*, pro-Union newspaper that had sprung up after the Civil War to counter the editorial views of the city's other three papers, enthusiastically supported the move. Of Horton, the paper wrote, "He is more than loyal; he is Republican—*believes* in equal rights for all men."

The transfer of power from Withers to Horton was cordial. Horton professed modesty. "My inclination and habits incline me to private rather than public life," he said. "Besides, the office to which I have been appointed is one which, at the present time, is surrounded with peculiar difficulties."

Withers defended his performance in office in a letter to General Shepherd and insisted that he was loyal to the U.S. government. He added, however: "I submit to the argument of the bayonet, and vacate the office."

Withers complained that he was being removed from office without trial or accusation.

"During my continuance in the office, I have worn no mask, have shunned no responsibilities, have feared no investigation," he wrote.

During Horton's tumultuous tenure as mayor, he tried to steer a middle course. He replaced nineteen police officers and hired the city's first black cops. He also replaced eighteen white laborers with black workers.

Horton's efforts to promote integration of newly freed blacks into society invited a predictable blowback from the city's formerly dominant white elite. The opposition newspapers kept up a steady barrage of attacks on the military-installed mayor, for example, spreading allegations that some of the black police officers were sleeping on the job.

In the case of Charles Archie Johnson, Horton's enemies found the ideal opportunity to turn the tables—and use the nation's new legal regime of black rights against him.

Johnson was an illiterate, one-legged former slave who worked as a newsboy for the *Mobile Tribune*. Police cited him three separate times for disorderly conduct in 1867. Presiding over the Mayor's Court, Horton twice ordered Johnson to leave the city, a common punishment for such offenses at the time. Both times, Johnson returned, however, and on the third charge of disorderly conduct—and public drunkenness and resisting arrest—Horton fined the defendant $50, sentenced him to thirty days in jail and ordered him to post a $300 peace bond.

Horton's critics pounced, accusing him of racism. The accusations led to his arrest on August 10, 1867, on a charge under the newly passed federal civil rights law. The *Mobile Advertiser and Register* called the charge "poetic justice" for the "Radical Military Mayor of Mobile."

After the trial, a jury deliberated for just five minutes before finding Horton guilty on December 20, 1867. U.S. district judge Richard Busteed imposed a fine of $250.

Horton eventually got a measure of revenge. He testified at Busteed's impeachment hearing in the House of Representatives in January 1869. Although that impeachment effort failed, Busteed resigned in 1874 after the House Judiciary Committee voted in favor of new impeachment charges.

Horton also enjoyed a political rehabilitation of his own. He won election in July 1868 to the office of probate judge. He also did another stint on the school board and served as collector of customs for the port from 1877 to 1885.

Horton died of heart failure on January 6, 1892. By that time, Southern Democrats long since had wrested back control of the city and the state, and Alabama had imposed what would be a nearly century-long system of rigid racial segregation.

Chapter 8

THE THEFT OF
THE COURTHOUSE

With the arrival of the seven o'clock hour, a caravan of thirteen double-team farm wagons shoved off from the town of Bay Minette and marched under cover of darkness toward the Baldwin County seat in Daphne. The men, some two dozen strong and armed with Winchester rifles and pistols, traveled in military-style formation.

E.J. Norris was one of them. Nineteen years old at the time, he had been recruited to help right what the good men of Bay Minette considered a grave injustice. He gripped his pistol nervously as the caravan got closer to Daphne.

To a passerby, the group may have resembled a company of soldiers, but this was no military mission. The men, under the command of James D. Hand, meant to break a legal stalemate over the proper location for the county seat by physically removing the courthouse from Daphne, a waterfront city situated across Mobile Bay from the city of Mobile. Among the men was state senator Daniel Dillon Hall, of the north Baldwin community of Tensaw.

The state legislature already had approved moving the county seat, and construction of a new courthouse had been completed. But a legal challenge brought by a group of Daphne residents was tied up in the courts. Hand set out to make the transfer a fait accompli.

After nearly seven hours, the caravan reached the outskirts of Daphne and set up camp between one and two o'clock in the morning on Friday, October 11, 1901. At daybreak, the men resumed their steady approach, stopping about a mile from the courthouse.

Hand led Company "C" to the jail behind the courthouse and presented Frederick Richardson, a black teenager accused of breaking into a home on Hurricane Bayou the day before, for incarceration. The teenager had been found drunk, sleeping on a pallet next to the daughter of the homeowner. The defendant had appeared in front of J.C. Day, a justice of the peace who, as it happened, also worked for Hand's lumber company.

When Sheriff George B. Bryant opened the jail cell to receive the prisoner, Hand and five other men rushed inside the cage. Bryant ordered the men to leave, and when they refused, he locked the door. Returning, he opened the door and tried again to clear the men out. Hand stepped outside, but the others stood firm.

Details of the raid vary. According to one version, Bryant again locked the cell door and left for Montrose, a community just to the south of Daphne. In another telling, the raiders distracted the sheriff with bogus reports of a murder in the south part of the county that sent him on a wild goose chase. Decades later, when E.J. Norris was a middle-aged mill foreman for a Mobile shipbuilding company, he told a newspaper reporter that the sheriff was in on the raid from the beginning.

"Sheriff George Bryant had arranged everything so all we had to do was walk into the courthouse and walk out with the records from Daphne and place them in the building," he said.

Either way, with the sheriff gone, Hand's men went quickly to work. After moving Richardson to a different part of the jail and securing him, they pulled out hatchets, crowbars, chisels and other tools and began to break down the jail. Meanwhile, Company "D" entered the courthouse and started removing desks, chairs, benches, books and vault doors. In a businesslike manner, the men cleared out everything from the probate judge's desk to the spittoons.

It took about five hours for the men to complete their work. With all thirteen wagons packed, the caravan took off for the new county courthouse in Bay Minette. Several men stayed behind to continue the dismantling. They ate dinner while they waited for the wagons to return.

The activity attracted a small crowd of Daphne residents, several of whom were upset at the spectacle of their town's central feature under assault. One resident declared it an invasion. Some shed tears as the wagons slowly made their way out of town.

"You may go, but in less time than a month we will have you bring them back," one resident said.

The men who remained to cut out jail cells and doors became convinced that an injunction was on its way from Mobile to halt their work. But an injunction was neither granted nor sought.

On Saturday night, after a seven-hour journey, more wagons pulled up to the courthouse to load the remaining items. The thieves packed up the most important papers in a large safe. By one account, probate judge Charles Hall carried the county seal, himself.

On the way back to Bay Minette, an axle on one of the wagons broke near Macedonia Baptist Church during services.

Some of the wagons reached Bay Minette that night. Other men camped for the night and made it back to the new county seat on Sunday, October 13.

Meanwhile, when Bryant returned to the courthouse on Saturday, October 12, he found it stripped and abandoned. He hopped a steamer for Mobile to consult with lawyers, later telling newspaper reporters that he would stop the "Bay Minette people" from molesting the court documents.

But by then, the furniture and paperwork of the courthouse were secure in the new building twenty-five miles north. If possession is nine-tenths of the law, as the old saying goes, Bay Minette had the upper hand for the four years of court wrangling that lay ahead.

Bay Minette greeted news of the courthouse theft with glee.

"Yes, we hoisted our Banner upon Daphne's soil and left her in sad mourning," boasted "one of the boys" in the raiding party.

An article in the *American Banner*, a weekly paper published in Bay Minette, bragged: "Ha! Ha! Ha! We are now living at the county seat."

The godfather of modern Bay Minette, it might be said, was James D. Hand. And his drive to make the city Baldwin's county seat was more than hometown civic pride. He had a potential personal fortune riding on it.

Hand had moved from Jemison, Alabama, settling in the D'Olive community just outside Bay Minette. He operated a sawmill and, in the last decade of the nineteenth century, purchased a nine-thousand-acre tract of land. He and J.C. Cameron formed the Hand-Cameron Lumber Company, which eventually became the Hand Lumber Company, close to the Louisville and Nashville Railroad.

The railroad's predecessor, the Mobile and Montgomery Railroad, had created Bay Minette's first subdivision in 1884. Hand had much bigger plans, which included residential districts, parks, a school and a business district surrounding a courthouse square. The key to the whole vision was the courthouse.

But the county could have only one seat of government, and since 1868—after yellow fever had decimated the previous county seat in Blakeley—that had been in Daphne. The official business of the county took place in a two-story brick courthouse constructed in 1886. It was the creation of noted Mobile architect Rudolph Benz, who also designed the Mobile County courthouse that opened three years later and the building that housed the Cotton Exchange and chamber of commerce.

A previous effort to move the county seat had failed a couple years earlier. But Hand was undeterred. He aggressively lobbied the state legislature to relocate the seat; a petition drive collected 1,344 signatures, or 1,115 if challenged names were removed. Even the lesser amount exceeded the 886 names that newspaper publisher Ernest Quincy Norton gathered for a counter petition.

Hand and his allies managed to win the support of Senator Hall and state representative George H. Hoyle of Daphne.

The debate in Montgomery in 1900 alarmed many Daphne residents. At times, emotions ran so hot that residents of Daphne and Bay Minette got into fistfights. J.J. McGill, a supporter of the relocation, and J.W. Creamer, chairman of the committee in favor of keeping the courthouse in Daphne, engaged in spirited debates in the local newspaper over the issue and politics in general.

In a letter to the editor of the *Daphne Times* published in December 1900, an "anxious voter" raised a host of objections.

"In the first place, how are they going to move it?" the writer asked. "Do you reckon they can dump the gosh blame thing on an ox cart and haul it to Bay Minette, or will Russell Dick be engaged to take it up there one brick at a time?"

The writer also pointed out that state law prohibited the sale of alcohol within six miles of a courthouse. What if someone were selling liquor on the road between Daphne and Bay Minette?

"For myself, I am against the scheme. Our courthouse now occupies a community position. It looms over Daphne like the Washington Monument in a grave yard," he wrote.

The building was constant companion to the homeless goats, razorbacks and other animals that grazed on the courthouse lawn. "Encouraging them in their wickedness, and as a consistent member of the church and democratic party, I am opposed to all such new fangled ideas," the writer finished with a flourish.

Hoyle took a particular beating. Some called him a traitor to his hometown, and others hung him in effigy. The *Daphne Times*, which supported the move, also took heat. The newspaper received threats to burn the printing office, forcing the company to post a night guard.

The bad blood prompted a libel lawsuit in April 1901 by Hoyle against Norton, who published a newspaper called the *Standard*. The complaint accused the newspaper of depicting Hoyle as engaging in "an illegal unpatriotic and dishonest proposition" by promising to defeat the bill relocating the county seat. Norton, according to the complaint, "tended and tried to produce a breach of the peace."

The county seat bill passed the legislature in February 1901, and Governor William J. Samford—two weeks before his death—refused to veto it, allowing it to become law. It decreed that the county seat should be relocated to Bay Minette and set up an elaborate procedure to pay for it. The act created a board of commissioners to oversee the relocation and sale of the Daphne courthouse. Hand was among the men tapped to serve on the commission, allowing him to personally oversee the transition that promised to make him rich.

With probate judge Charles Hall presiding, the Commissioners Court—the equivalent of a county commission today—voted the following Monday to donate $2,500 for a new jail and courthouse.

Meanwhile, at its first meeting, the board of commissioners elected Hand as its chairman.

On March 2, 1901, a state law took effect directing the Baldwin County probate judge to serve as trustee for a school being authorized for white children at the location of the Daphne courthouse. The school was to purchase the courthouse for not more than $6,000.

Hand and his wife, Mittie, along with Hand Lumber Company, donated two and a half acres in Bay Minette for the courthouse project. The board accepted the offer. He also contributed $1,600.

At the end of March, the board of commissioners voted to sell the Daphne courthouse. It selected Lockwood and Smith of Montgomery to design the new building. The Louisville and Nashville Railroad, which desired a county seat on its line between Mobile and the state capital in Montgomery, offered to provide free transportation to the architects, as well as free freight services. The total contribution was valued at $1,600.

Later, the board awarded the $21,000 construction contract to F.M. Dobson for the jail and courthouse. The contractor began work on the site a few days after the May 23 vote.

Gus B. Stapleton, who ran a drinking house called Gus's Place in Daphne, and several others sued that month to halt the project. Hand and the other defendants responded on July 3, asking the judge to rule that the plaintiffs were not entitled to any relief even if the allegations they made were true.

Thomas H. Smith of the Chancery Court in Mobile, with jurisdiction over Baldwin County, took the request under advisement. Meanwhile, work proceeded in Bay Minette. The F&M Masonic Lodge 498 laid the cornerstone during a Fourth of July celebration. Hand conveyed land north of the railroad on July 8.

Smith would not rule until December 3, 1901, ultimately rejecting the defendants' request to toss the case. They appealed that ruling to the Alabama Supreme Court. But by then, the courthouse raid already had taken place.

———•———

Charles Hall, the probate judge in 1901, traced his family tree to the beginning of the United States. A branch of the family were cousins of George Washington, and one member of the clan served on the general's staff during the Revolutionary War.

A prior Charles Hall came to Baldwin County in about 1783, when it was still part of West Florida under Spanish rule. He married Mary Byrne in 1803. Five years later, the couple settled on the "Honey Cut" three miles north of the old Hall home and built a mill there in 1812.

He had three sons, including Joseph Hall, who became a state representative. The last son of Charles and Mary Hall, also named Charles, bore a son named Charles in 1854. His son, the fourth to be named Charles Hall, moved to Daphne and served as postmaster from 1888 to 1891. He ran successfully for probate judge and served twelve years.

Upon his death in 1927, the *Baldwin Times* praised his long years of public service: "No man ever served Baldwin with greater earnestness of purpose, unalloyed sincerity, and fidelity to duty, that always marked his services."

Two of his grandchildren told the *Mobile Register* in 2001 that the judge was innocent of the historical accusations. They said that their aunt—Hall's daughter, who was a young girl in 1901—recalled a group of men coming to the house and demanding the keys to the courthouse. Hall refused and asked the men to take care of the records if they did break into the building.

E.J. Norris, the nineteen-year-old who participated in the raid, offered a benign description of Hall's participation.

"After we had moved the courthouse, there was nothing more for the judge to do but come down to Bay Minette and hold court," he said.

Whether or not Hall supported the theft, he at the very least had advance knowledge of it. The last document that the judge recorded in Daphne was a deed conveying property from Charles O. Elstrom and his wife to Andrew Tallberg. Hall did not record other deeds filed in Daphne on October 7 until October 16, after the courthouse had reopened in Bay Minette.

The courthouse raid proved politically costly to the county's elected officials. Hall and all of the members of the Commissioners Court lost their reelection bids.

The ruling from the Supreme Court on the defendants' appeal did not come until sixteen months—to the day—after Hand and his men set off for Daphne to retrieve the courthouse furniture and files. Writing for the court on February 10, 1903, Justice John R. Tyson ruled that the law authorizing the county seat transfer did not violate the state constitution.

The statute was somewhat contradictory. On the one hand, it unconditionally declared that Bay Minette was the new county seat. On the other hand, it stated that the move would not occur until funds had been raised and a determination made that the construction could be financed without raising the tax rate.

"We do not think it can be gainsaid that it was the general purpose of the Legislature to authorize the building of the courthouse and jail at Bay Minette provided it could be done without increasing the tax rate of the county," Tyson wrote.

The high court sent the case back to Chancery Court, and the state legislature also passed another law explicitly ratifying all previous actions related to the transfer. It became law on March 4, 1903. But that was far from the end of the case.

Gus Stapleton and the other plaintiffs amended the complaint in an effort to take the Supreme Court decision into account. The new complaint alleged that the board of commissioners failed to comply with the requirement of the statute to certify that the courthouse and jail could be constructed without raising taxes.

The defendants again asked the judge to throw out the suit, and Chancellor Smith again ruled against them. But this time, on July 21, 1904, the Supreme Court affirmed the judge's decision. It ruled without issuing an opinion, but Justice Tyson published a dissent arguing that the legislature must have known that tax revenues from a single year could not have been sufficient to build a courthouse and jail.

"The logical result from what we have said is that the debt could be distributed for several years so as to be paid out of the revenue of the county during those years without any increase of the then existing tax rate," he wrote.

The case returned to Chancery Court once again. On August 21, 1905, both sides agreed on the facts, leaving Smith to rule on the law. On August 31, he ruled that the law authorizing the relocation of the county seat never took effect except for the provision qualifying the board of commissioners to appraise the Daphne property and raise money for the new courthouse. He ordered the county treasurer not to make any more payments related to the project.

Circuit judge Samuel B. Browne on September 11 ordered Sheriff James M. Armstrong to hold a full term of court in Daphne. When the sheriff refused, Browne ordered his arrest. When the coroner refused to take the sheriff into custody, the judge asked the governor to send in the state militia.

The defendants appealed Smith's ruling, and for the third time in four years, the case once again was before the Alabama Supreme Court. A combination of retirements and a law expanding the court from five to seven members shifted the composition to a more favorable posture from the perspective of Hand and his supporters.

This time, the high court overruled Smith on December 19, 1905. It dissolved the injunction and ratified what by now was the status quo. Court sessions and county government business had been held in Bay Minette for more than four years at that point.

"It is shown, from the evidence in the case, that said courthouse commissioners have legally and properly ascertained the facts necessary to make the act effectual, and have properly proceeded in accordance with the powers conferred upon them to have the buildings referred to in said act erected," Justice Robert Tennent Simpson wrote in the court's opinion.

For the Daphne boosters, the end of the line had come. They had exhausted all legal remedies, and a nighttime raid of their own to retake the courthouse seemed farfetched.

The "courthouse theft" and its subsequent ratification by the courts had profound and long-lasting effects for both Bay Minette and the man who engineered the transfer. Eight months after the final Supreme Court decision, Hand sold his Bay Minette holdings to Hampton D. Ewing, president of the Bay Minette Land Company. Hand made a tidy profit, and Bay Minette developed much like he originally had envisioned.

Several lawyers picked up from Daphne and moved their offices to Bay Minette to be close to the courthouse. The *Daphne Times* also moved its printing offices to Bay Minette, changing its name to the *Baldwin Times*, and publishing its first edition on October 24, 1901.

The courthouse remains in Bay Minette today. The "theft" captured the popular imagination and continues to resonate. An artist's depiction of the event hangs in the Bay Minette post office. In 2001, Daphne officials included a mock crime report among items buried in a time capsule to commemorate the centennial of Bay Minette's status as the county seat.

Daphne, meanwhile, survived the blow of losing the county seat. Its proximity to Mobile, combined with a pair of crossings over Mobile Bay constructed later in the century, helped make the city a bedroom community of commuters. Today, it is Baldwin County's largest city.

Chapter 9

BOARDWALK EMPIRE OF
THE SOUTH

$\mathcal{D}$uring the week of November 12, 1923, dozens of federal agents who had been preparing for this moment for more than five months, fanned out across Mobile in a well-orchestrated raid that swept up booze from homes and businesses. For days, trucks kept rolling up to the Custom House and Federal Building on St. Francis Street with crates of scotch, bourbon, rum and Benedictine.

Agents collected ten thousand quarts on the first day, including 415 cases from a single address on Conception Street. According to the *Mobile Register*, the government rented nearly every large truck in the city to assist the operation.

Eventually, authorities determined that the third floor of the building was not sturdy enough to withstand the weight of the contraband. So John Murphy, who was overseeing the raiding agents, ordered the construction of a metal cage to contain the stacked cases in the alley between the Federal Building and the First National Bank Building.

Even in a city that flouted Prohibition so energetically, the final haul was staggering: liquor valued at $100,000, a sum equivalent to nearly $1.4 million in 2015 money.

Izzy Einstein, one of two agents of the U.S. Prohibition Unit who racked up the most arrests in the early days of America's experiment with radical temperance, said he had "never seen such a variety of booze."

The feds spared no precaution in protecting the loot. They surrounded the contraband with an electrified, barbed-wire fence and outfitted four

During the week of November 1923, federal agents fanned out across Mobile and seized thousands of quarts of illicit liquor throughout the city. The underground liquor ring was the most brazen in a long history of opposition to Prohibition. *Doy Leave McCall Rare Book and Manuscript Library.*

guards with sawed-off shotguns. The *New York Times*, reporting on the raids, drew comparisons to the trench warfare of World War I.

"A ghoulish aspect was given to the warlike scene tonight when red lamps were also supplied the guards," the article stated.

If the scope of the raids was surprising to Mobilians, it likely did not compare to the shock they felt when a federal grand jury concluded its work just before Christmas—117 indictments reading like a who's who of the city's most distinguished fathers.

There was Mobile County sheriff Paul G. Cazalas and his immediate predecessor, William "Willie" Holcombe, who was in the state legislature at the time. Also indicted were Mobile Police chief Patrick J. O'Shaughnessy, Mobile County commissioner A.G. Ward, "Mr. Mardi Gras" Alfred Staples, local attorney Percy H. Kearns and J. B. Connaughton, a Hamilton, Ohio lawyer who had lived briefly in Mobile.

At the head of it all, according to prosecutors, was Frank W. Boykin. One of Alabama's most colorful political figures of the twentieth century, a man who would go on to serve fourteen terms in Congress, Boykin in the 1920s was a prominent businessman. That business, prosecutors alleged, was running a sophisticated operation importing liquor from

Cuba through Mobile Bay and smuggling it to various parts of the ostensibly dry country.

"This liquor scandal will not only involve a number of ordinary bootleggers but probably some of the 'Master Minds' and higher ups," the *Mobile Register* promised its readers.

Mobile's top federal prosecutor, who directed the whiskey raids, told reporters that "gambling fixers" had offered him a $150,000 bribe to slow the investigation.

———•———

The federal government had its hands full enforcing the Eighteenth Amendment in cities large and small across the country. But perhaps nowhere was Prohibition so brazenly ignored as in Mobile.

The city had more practice at it than most.

Alabama led most of the country into the Prohibition movement. The state began cracking down on alcohol in the first decade of the century. Despite pockets of resistance, the largely Protestant state mostly supported that effort.

Mobile did not.

With its port, its large Catholic population and its history of frivolity, Mobile stood apart from the rest of the state. It acquired a reputation as a "loose" city in the nineteenth century, and municipal leaders were not always aggressive in combating that impression.

In 1896, Mobile passed an ordinance confining "houses of ill fame" to a small section of the northwest corner of the city. Outside this area, women could be fined fifty dollars in the Recorder's Court if convicted of prostitution.

Lax morals, perhaps, contributed to health problems. From 1885 to 1896, only Savannah, Georgia, had a higher mortality rate. In 1896, alone, 142 people in Mobile died from tuberculosis.

Business leaders expressed concern in 1907 that prostitutes were operating well beyond the restricted zone, especially during Mardi Gras season. Lawyer Frederick Bromberg led a call for a crackdown.

A coalition of businessmen, educators and ministers renewed the call for tighter regulations between 1913 and 1919. But rampant prostitution persisted into the 1920s.

Corruption also was nothing new for the Azalea City. Between 1913 and 1917, several police officers faced charges of accepting bribes, brandishing pistols in public and consorting with prostitutes. The police department dismissed several officers in 1916 following a public outcry over reports that they had been with black prostitutes.

In 1909, Mobile County sheriff Frank Cazalas Sr. was impeached and removed from office for neglect during an incident in which a mob entered the jail and lynched a black prisoner accused of killing a white deputy.

Against this backdrop, anti-alcohol reformers in the state clashed against its libertine city on the Gulf coast. City leaders and ordinary citizens, alike, chaffed at a series of alcohol control measures passed by the legislature in 1907. This included a "local option" law that gave wet counties the option of banning alcohol sales. (It was a one-way street, though; dry counties could not decide to allow alcohol sales).

The regulation built on a law passed during the 1898–99 legislative session allowing local governments to set up publicly run dispensaries to limit the consumption of alcohol and drive private sellers out of business. Mobile County was among those exempted from that statute, however.

The success of those regulations was debatable. In 1900, 116,094 gallons of whiskey had been distilled in Alabama. By 1907, the annual total had grown to 214,255. Governor Braxton Bragg Comer, an ardent prohibition supporter, pushed for stronger regulations. He received dozens of letters from Mobilians urging him to fight one-size-fits-all proposals that would impose alcohol restrictions on unwilling counties.

"Mobile has survived epidemics of Yellow Fever, overcome the devastation by storms, and depression caused by financial panics, but I believe prohibition placed upon her without her people having a direct voice in the matter would be the greatest blow to her progress and prosperity the city has ever had," wrote Albert Sidney Lyons, who at the time was simultaneously Mobile's mayor pro tem and a state representative.

Lyons also had personal and professional reasons for opposing prohibition. He was the leading stockholder in the Mobile Brewery. His ties to the alcohol business were hardly unusual for the city's political elite. Between 1897 and 1910, at least three members of the Mobile General Council were wholesale grocers or liquor agents. Mobile newspaper editor Erwin Craighead cited those special interests in a letter to the governor: "I think you will find, upon inquiry, that brewing interests are responsible in this state for many of the evils," he wrote to the governor.

Craighead's newspaper, the *Mobile Register*, made arguments in 1907 that are strikingly similar to the ones that advocates of legalized marijuana make today.

"Prohibition in a city with Mobile's attitude toward liquor, would not give relief," the paper stated. "It would mean unlicensed sale, underground sale; instead of open sale; bad whiskey sold for good whiskey; and a weakening of the moral status of the community."

On another occasion, the *Register* argued it would be "an act of tyranny" to force prohibition on Mobile.

Lyons warned that banning alcohol sales would hurt the schools, cost the city tax revenue and cause its port to lose business to wet New Orleans. Peter J. Hamilton, a local attorney and historian, also cited the impact on tax revenue for education.

"The Mobile school system was not only the first in the state but the beginning of the state system," he wrote to Comer in November 1907. "It does not become the state now to repay the debt with ingratitude."

Developer William W. Thompson wrote to the governor in September 1907 explaining that prohibition would impede his efforts to settle the farmlands of Baldwin County across the bay from Mobile. He wrote that he recently had returned from a trip to Chicago, where he was trying to entice immigrants to move to Alabama.

"I believe that if this law was passed, it would keep out many thousand [*sic*] of these people and retard the growth of the state as much as anything that could possibly be done," he wrote.

The state's goal, Thompson continued, should be temperance, not prohibition.

"The Swedes and Germans are all drinkers of wine and beer but very few of them are drunkards," he wrote.

Mobile mayor Patrick J. Lyons—no relation to A.S. Lyons—led a delegation to Montgomery to lobby against the prohibition bill in November 1907. On the eve of the vote, Bank of Mobile president M.J. McDermott wired state senator Max Hamburger that "unless anti-prohibitionists win today please give notice that Mobile is prepared to secede from the State of Alabama and organize a home government and cease to be dominated by our country cousins, whose efforts to paralyze Mobile will not be tolerated."

Mobile did not break away from Alabama. But opposition continued even after the legislature adopted the alcohol reforms. So opposed to Comer's liquor program were Mobilians that Hamburger in 1908 suggested to an aide that the governor's safety might be in jeopardy if he attended a planned Civil War reunion in the city.

To be sure, anti-prohibition sentiment in Mobile was not unanimous. In 1909, the virulently anti-Catholic Junior Order United American Merchants established a Mobile chapter.

Several prominent ministers and others formed the Law and Order League, which supported efforts to limit or ban the sale of alcohol. Comer gave the organization $100 from the state treasury and $25 of his own money. He also empowered it to help enforce alcohol laws.

The league hired attorneys Aubrey W. Boyles and Moses Kohn, as well as a private detective to help county solicitor Nicholas E. Stallworth gather evidence against liquor dealers. Boyles, as the federal district attorney two decades later, would be the man to bring criminal charges in the blockbuster liquor raids of 1923.

Some private citizens expressed support in letters to Comer and urged him to go further and ban other vices.

"Our mayor is a Catholic and you know what that means and the whole trend of thought along these lines in a Catholic city is one of tolerance," wrote Belle Peterson Inge, whose husband was a physician and council member. "They gamble at their church fairs so of course they see no harm in it."

Craighead, the newspaper editor, agreed that the city's heritage diverged from the rest of the state and that it had a profound impact on its politics.

"We are somewhat Frenchified down here and take our manners and customs from the old-time inhabitants," he wrote.

It's clear that local politicians were not far from where their constituents stood on the issue. Opposition from Mobile did little to quell anti-prohibition fervor across the state, however. Most areas seemed eager for, or at least accepting of, statewide alcohol restrictions that were set to take effect in January 1909.

The rest of Alabama did not express much sympathy or tolerance for Mobile's complaints. "Mobile is no worse off than other parts of the state and will have to take her medicine," the *Birmingham Ledger* wrote in an article quoted by the *Mobile Daily Herald* in March 1908. The same article quoted the *Opelika News*: "The spirit of rebellion really seems rife in Mobile. It is known to be a city of great wealth, and such displays of countenancing lawlessness, such admission of inability to meet her obligations is shameful."

The *Herald* defended its city. "It is not a crime to denounce sumptuary laws or to test the validity of laws before the courts."

Comer announced in July 1909 that even tighter restrictions were needed: "The statewide prohibition law has been found inadequate of enforcement, and evasions of law have been many and apparently easy."

The lawmakers, in a special session that month, outlawed the manufacture and sale of beverages with as little as one half of one percent of alcohol. It also provided for the impeachment of local authorities who failed to enforce the law.

Attempts to codify the ban in the state constitution failed later that year, however, and the state repealed the harsh law in 1911. In its place, the legislature gave counties and cities the power to regulate saloons by setting up excise commissions to eradicate "blind tigers" and "negro dives." The focus on drinking by blacks was particularly strong, with roots dating to the slave days. The Ku Klux Klan was a key part of the anti-alcohol coalition in the early twentieth century.

The easing of restrictions proved short-lived, however. Prohibition supporters eventually wrested full control of the state legislature and in 1915 imposed a full ban on alcohol—over the veto of Governor Charles Henderson. The law took effect on July 1, forcing the closure of alcohol businesses that day. Alabama became the driest state in the union a full five years before Prohibition became the law of the land with the Eighteenth Amendment.

—•—

Banning alcohol in the law is one thing. Enforcing it is quite another.

Throughout the early twentieth century, Mobile officials pursued alcohol enforcement with less-than-enthusiastic vigor.

John Drago—who would go on to serve as sheriff—warned Comer in November 1908 that a new law taking effect the next year banning the sale of alcohol after nine o'clock would be ineffectual without cooperative local authorities. He lobbied against the appointment of Joseph McNamara as jury commissioner, noting that the man's brother operated drinking establishments supported by Negroes.

"Conditions in Mobile in regard to the sale of liquor after 9:00 P.M. is not improved and intoxicating beverages are going to be sold here after January 1st, unless the municipal and sheriff authorities…become active," he wrote. "Without the assistance of the Mayor, sheriff, and jury commissioners, very little can be done."

Pat Lyons, who first became Mobile's mayor in 1904 and dominated city politics for a generation, did enforce the state's nine o'clock closing laws on saloons but not much else. And within two years of taking effect, even that law no longer had force in the city.

"No matter what you hear," the Law and Order League's Boyles and Kohn wrote to the governor in 1909, "Mobile is still a wet city."

Elliott G. Rickarby, in a letter to a friend in October 1909, complained of alcohol violations in a sailors' saloon and hotel near the waterfront.

"In fact, lower Conti Street, where this place is, is a place where no lady of my family would go unescorted by a man and no man of my acquaintance would take a lady if he could help it," he wrote.

Even when police did make arrests, they rarely stuck in court. In 1910, two hundred arrests for liquor violations had been made, but not a single case was tried.

Comer was exasperated.

"You know, I am depending upon you, not the City government," the governor wrote to Drago, who by then was sheriff.

Drago complied, issuing twenty warrants for liquor violations, including prominent restaurateur Charles Schimff. But he was cleared of all charges and got a standing ovation as he left the courtroom.

Boyles, in a 1909 letter to Comer, questioned the commitment of Judge Oliver J. Semmes and juries to enforcing liquor laws.

"The jurors of criminal court of this city fail to measure up to the standard of citizenship found in the country as a whole," he wrote.

H.H. Mitchel was blunter. "Judge Semmes permits men to sit as jurors who are bar keepers, and men who swear that they are 'opposed to the enforcement of the law,'" he wrote to Comer. "This makes it impossible for us to get convictions."

In 1908, Drago had complained to Comer that Senator Hamburger was unfit for office. He wrote that Hamburger, who also was jury commissioner, had spent time in a state asylum in Tuscaloosa "the result of a protracted spree" and hardly had returned before he got drunk again and spent time in jail on two separate occasions.

Drago urged Comer to replace Hamburger as jury commissioner with a local named John Case.

———◆———

Mobile was no more receptive to the notion of giving up its liquor on the eve of national Prohibition than it was in the early part of the century.

Prominent Mobilians kept up appearances, though.

Some of the men who would become embroiled in the great liquor trials of the 1920s insisted that they were doing their best to stamp out alcohol smuggling.

Bart B. Chamberlain, the Mobile County solicitor—a vocal prohibition opponent during his time in the legislature—wrote to pro-prohibition Alabama governor Thomas E. Kilby in 1919 that he needed more resources to stop the law breaking. He passed on a tip from a federal agent about a large shipment of liquor likely to come from New Orleans later in the summer.

Chamberlain—who would play a key role in resisting the federal government's crackdown on rum running in Mobile a few years later—asked Kilby for $100 to hire a boat and crew to patrol the Mississippi Sound. He reported that local law enforcement authorities recently had intercepted a shipment of one hundred sixty-eight cases of whiskey and fifteen cases of beer.

"We are making an honest effort to enforce the prohibition law in this county and are meeting with success," he wrote.

Chamberlain also reported that he had been unable to make a case against taxi drivers thought to be hauling liquor.

Kilby approved Chamberlain's request.

Sheriff Holcombe, who would be named in the 1923 indictment, defended himself in 1919 against allegations of lax enforcement. He disputed a citizen's allegations of rampant smuggling.

"There is undoubtedly whiskey somewhere in Mobile County, but I do not believe that there is anything like the amount stipulated, viz; 1000 cases," he wrote to Kilby.

Holcombe wrote that his department had made a large seizure in June and had broken up six whiskey stills, although there was evidence in only two of the cases. He blamed complaints against him on upset felons and a sore loser candidate for sheriff.

"Press reports, as well as Court Records, will show that my department has been very active in the enforcement of the Prohibition Law," he wrote.

By the early 1920s, Mobile's underground liquor trade was as lucrative as ever, and many of the city's leading officer-holders were sharing in the profits. The *Mobile Register* reported in 1920 that, "Every creek in the county, practically, has yielded a still."

But like elsewhere in the United States during the Prohibition era, the trade could be violent.

In February 1921, Mobile County sheriff's deputies showed up to arrest Malcolm McLaurin on a charge of selling prohibited liquors. The suspect's father, a sixty-year-old crippled gunsmith named Dan McLaurin, charged out of a store on Davis Avenue and argued that he was the man police should be arresting. Deputy Earl Easterling decided to take McLaurin up on that offer.

During the confrontation, McLaurin pulled out a revolver and shot the deputy dead. Another officer shot McLaurin. He contracted smallpox at City Hospital and died in a city pesthouse before he could be tried for Easterling's murder.

Not even liquor-related murders could top what Mobile would experience from 1923 to 1925. The liquor raids from November 1923 made an almost unthinkable number of people criminal defendants—117 in all. Boyles, the United States district attorney who helped plan the raids, had by then had a long career fighting liquor violations. In addition to his earlier work for the Law and Order League, he had shut down, as a special prosecutor, the brewery run by Mobile's Lyons family.

Among the defendants was Frank Boykin, charged with bribing Boyles. Boykin was well connected politically—a close associate of the brother of disgraced former U.S. attorney general Harry M. Daugherty—and it did not take long to strike back. Chamberlain, Mobile County's top prosecutor, arrested Boyles the day after a federal grand jury handed up the indictment in the liquor case. He charged Boyles with trying to improperly influence two state law enforcement officers.

That forced Boyles to recuse himself from the federal case in December 1923. For his replacement, U.S. attorney general Harlan Fiske Stone tapped little-known Birmingham prosecutor Hugo Black. An ambitious young lawyer, Black had cut his teeth in the war on alcohol as Jefferson County's prosecutor, a position he used in 1916 to go after newspapers that printed ads for liquor businesses.

The reputed head of a large, underground liquor empire was Frank W. Boykin, a Mobile businessman who would go on to a long and colorful career in Congress. *Doy Leale McCall Rare Book and Manuscript Library.*

A member of the Ku Klux Klan, Black would parlay his role in the Mobile liquor trials into a successful bid for the U.S. Senate and eventually a seat on the U.S. Supreme Court.

Kearns, the Mobile lawyer, was the first to stand trial. Prosecutors alleged that he was the "bag man" for the "protection money" paid to bootleggers. With the backing of the city's law enforcement establishment, the whiskey ring sought to control the market by forcing black market alcohol businesses to buy their product from them exclusively. Testimony in court indicated that an undercover federal agent had received money from Kearns at a room inside Mobile's Cawthon Hotel off Bienville Square while investigators monitored the meeting through a peephole.

But the jury deadlocked, sending prosecutors back to the drawing board. Black responded with a bold strategy of putting Boykin and seventy other defendants on trial for a single charge of conspiracy to violate the Volstead Act, the law Congress passed to enforce the Prohibition amendment.

Several minor players in the conspiracy pleaded guilty, but most of the major defendants went to trial. On April 28, 1924, the courtroom had difficulty accommodating the large number of defendants and lawyers as the trial got under way. Many of the most recognizable members of the city's bar were represented.

The trial took on a circus-like atmosphere, straining the ability of U.S. District Court judge Robert T. Ervin to maintain order in the courtroom. On one occasion, he fined two defendants and put them in jail for ten days after they got into a fistfight during a break in the trial. On another, the judge fined William Holcombe $250 for mumbling an expletive in court.

"Don't you cuss me, Willie Holcombe," said Harry French, a corrupt former law enforcement officer under indictment for murder who was working undercover for the Justice Department.

According to local legend, Boykin went so far as to eat a telegram from Washington rather than allow it to be introduced into evidence. The tale has been repeated by generations of Mobile lawyers and appears in several books. Greg Smith, the son of Boykin's defense attorney, Harry Hardy Smith, told the *Mobile Register* in 2001 that his father confirmed the incident was true.

But the telegram-eating incident did not make contemporaneous news coverage, and various retellings of the story did not indicate what damning evidence the telegram contained.

At any rate, the case against Boykin was weak. At the end of the prosecution case, Ervin tossed out the charges against him and nine other defendants.

The Holcombe brothers were among thirty-three other defendants who won acquittal on May 22, 1924. But the jury did return guilty verdicts against Kearns, Chief O'Shaughnessy and nine other defendants.

Black got a second crack at Boykin and Willie Holcombe in February 1925. A pair of smugglers who earlier had been convicted implicated Boykin, the Holcombe brothers and Alfred Staples. In addition to the indictment on charges of conspiracy to bribe federal officials, they each faced a new substantive bribery count.

Witnesses testified that smugglers transferred tar barrels packed with liquor from Cuban ships twelve miles off the U.S. coast and then shipped them up the Mobile River to McIntosh north of Mobile, where they were stored in a warehouse owned by Boykin's brother. Frank Boykin paid a dollar and a half per barrel and kept thousands of dollars to pay off federal agents. He also collected five dollars above the going price in protection money, according to the testimony.

"There was really a rum ring, and I was a part of it," bootlegger Dan Jemison testified. "Frank Boykin talked me into it. He talked us all into it."

Jemison testified that he called other conspirators in May 1923.

James Daves testified that he was supposed to sell the liquor in New Orleans, Chicago or elsewhere. "Yessir, I did. I got rid of a lot of it," he responded to a question from the prosecutor.

Daves testified that the big buyers were supposed to offer protection.

"But when the federal men came, they took all my stock and I got thrown in the brig," he told the jury. "Not much protection to that."

A Chicago man named Ike Cohen testified that he helped Boykin set up a trainload of whiskey to be sent from Mobile to the Windy City.

Despite the evidence, the jury found the defendants not guilty.

The very next day, Boykin, the Holcombes and Ohio lawyer J.B. Connaughton went on trial one more time, this time on a charge of bribing a federal agent. Boyles, the federal district attorney who had bowed out of the case after his own criminal indictment, testified that Boykin offered to pay $100,000 for advance information on the raids.

"He asked me if I had an automobile. I told him 'no,'" Boyles testified. "He said, 'Aubrey, it does not look dignified for a United States attorney not to have an automobile. If you say so, I can have one delivered to your home tomorrow.'"

Boyles also testified that Boykin told him that a $5 million loan to the Republican National Committee by industrialist Andrew Mellon was to be repaid with protection for liquor prosecution.

At the end of the trial, Black finally got his man. The jury handed down guilty verdicts for Boykin, as well as Willie Holcombe, although the panel deadlocked on the other defendants.

The case reverberated in Mobile for several years. Although he had not been convicted of criminal charges, Sheriff Paul Cazalas now faced state impeachment charges, prompting him to resign.

A federal judge agreed to transfer Mobile County solicitor Bart Chamberlain's criminal charges against Boyles to U.S. District Court. Those charges ultimately were dropped in August 1924, and Boyles won reinstatement to his old job that same month. Boyles beat back an effort to disbar him two years later.

When federal prosecutors cracked down on illegal alcohol, Mobile County solicitor Bart B. Chamberlain struck back, obtaining an indictment against U.S. district attorney Aubrey Boyles on a charge of trying to improperly influence state law enforcement officers. *Doy Leale McCall Rare Book and Manuscript Library.*

But the damage to his professional career was done. After the U.S. Senate refused to reconfirm him as U.S. district attorney in 1926—after as many as sixty members of the Mobile Bar Association signed a statement opposing him and Judge Robert Ervin led a delegation to Washington to speak against him—he ran unsuccessfully for Congress as a Republican.

That same year, a federal appeals court decided that the indictment against Boykin and Holcombe was excessively vague and overturned their bribery convictions.

That also was the same year that Hugo Black won his first election to the U.S. Senate.

Boykin, meanwhile, won election to the House in 1934 and served until 1963. Another criminal prosecution bookended his long political career. He went on trial in Baltimore on influence-peddling charges. The very day of his arrest was "Frank Boykin Day" in Mobile to celebrate the congressman's long career, and city officials chose to press ahead with the ceremony despite the scandal.

A judge sentenced the seventy-eight-year-old to federal prison. But President Lyndon Johnson pardoned him, and he never spent a day behind bars. He died a year later.

Chapter 10

THE BATTLE HOUSE HONOR KILLING

It was an easy one-block walk from Henry Morton Butler Jr.'s real estate office to the famed Battle House Hotel on Royal Street on August 22, 1932. Butler was curious about the conversation he had had with a Mr. Johnson wanting to talk about some investments. He had never heard of the man, but Mr. Johnson dropped the name of a mutual acquaintance, Ed Overton, relating that his brother suggested a meeting.

So the twenty-seven-year-old man from a well-connected Mobile family made his way to the stately building in the heart of downtown Mobile a little after five o'clock in the afternoon and took the elevator to the fifth floor, where he spotted a man exiting Room 552.

"Are you H.M. Butler?" asked the man, who stood at five feet, nine inches, and wore his dark, brown hair just above his light, brown eyes.

A slightly smaller man with light brown hair walked out of the hotel room just behind him; Butler recognized that man as Samuel Dyson, the brother-in-law of the young woman with whom he had had a fling before his own marriage in December 1930. Sam, in fact, had stopped Butler on the street that morning to try to arrange a meeting between Butler and the woman's husband, Sam's brother Raymond Dyson.

"Sam, I know you," Butler said, as the two men ushered him into the room.

"I don't know you," he said to Raymond.

The Dyson brothers had been at the hotel since one o'clock that afternoon hoping to confront Butler about the terminated affair. Raymond had called twice, at 1:30 p.m. and again an hour later. Both times, he had been told Mr.

The Battle House Hotel in downtown Mobile was the site of historic events and hosted prominent guests. It also was the site of a grisly murder in the summer of 1932. *Doy Leale McCall Rare Book and Manuscript Library.*

Butler was not in the office. On the third call, at about 4:30 p.m., Raymond left a message to call a "Mr. Johnson" and, a short while later, had the phone conversation that lured Butler to the hotel.

But nearly an hour had passed, and the Dyson brothers were about to give up hope.

"I don't think he will come," Sam told his brother.

Sam Dyson carried a small suitcase to the car, which was parked on St. Francis and Water Streets about a block from the hotel, and returned to the room. Raymond gathered his belongings and turned into the hallway. That is when he spied Butler coming from the elevator.

The Dysons escorted Butler into the hotel room. "You have done me a great wrong," Raymond said as he closed the door. "I doubt the legitimacy of my son, and I want to know. I came here to find out from you when your relations with my wife commenced."

"None of your damn business," Butler replied.

Raymond Dyson needed no stronger provocation to violence. He swung hard with a closed fist, delivering a blow to Butler's jaw so forceful that it knocked the man's glasses off his face and a straw hat from his head. Raymond bruised his knuckles against Butler's teeth as the hapless victim hit his head against the bed.

Butler tried to fight back, flailing at his aggressor's stomach and face. But Raymond never relinquished the upper hand. Butler's head slammed against the radiator and then Sam, who had been standing between the beds, helped his brother drag the man into the hotel room's bathroom in the northwest corner of the room.

What happened next—at least in the recounting by prosecutors at Raymond's murder trial later that year—was a two-on-one beating in which Butler never had a chance. One of the brothers smashed a heavy glass candlestick against the back of Butler's head, resulting in a small bump on his skull. They ripped his trousers and tied his hands with his own belt so tightly that it left marks on the victim's wrists.

As Sam restrained Butler, Raymond unleashed a barrage of blows that blackened Butler's left eye and bloodied his face. Butler tried to yell for help, but Raymond retrieved his handkerchief and shoved it down the man's throat. He then picked up a three-legged stool and slammed it against his head.

Butler slumped unconscious, his feet pointing toward the bedroom. The brothers wrapped a towel around his mouth, gulped cups of water, and quickly left the hotel without checking out or returning the key.

On their way back home to Fairhope, a small town on the other side of Mobile Bay, Raymond asked his brother to turn off into the Mobile Steel Company, where they had spent the morning discussing a bid they intended to make the following day to construct four houses at Maxwell Field in Montgomery. Raymond placed an anonymous call to the hotel to get help for the beaten man, Sam Dyson would later testify, in a way that would not draw the attention of police so that "this thing would not be broadcast to the newspapers."

L.N. Calhoun, the hotel's room clerk, sent bellboy Jerry Jones to check on the room at about 5:15 p.m. Jones returned and said he heard snoring from inside the chamber.

Concerned that perhaps the earlier warning had not been taken seriously, Raymond suggested making another phone call once they reached Daphne, a town just north of their home in Fairhope. Sam Dyson walked into Dryer's drugstore between 5:20 p.m. and 5:30 p.m., picked up the telephone and asked the operator to dial Dexter 4100, the Battle House Hotel's exchange.

"Get the house physician or some other physician up to Room 552 and keep it quiet," he told the hotel clerk.

Then the Dyson boys drove to the home of their father, Marmaduke Dyson, who made one last follow-up call to the hotel a little after six o'clock.

The clerk sent the hotel's detective, A.N. Stafford, to investigate at about 6:30 p.m. When he arrived, the room key was in the closed but unlocked door. He knocked three times and, when he heard no response, walked inside to find the mirror on a dresser turned up at an angle, as if someone had arranged it for an ambush so that the victim could not see anyone approaching from behind.

Stafford saw the straw hat between the bed and the radiator, shattered glass on the floor, blood near the foot of the bed and Butler's body in the bathroom. Blood dropped from the edge of the stool, which was turned upside down in the middle of the bedroom floor.

Stafford summoned the hotel's assistant manager and sent for the house physician, Dr. Sheldon H. Stephens. The stylish hotel was now a crime scene.

———•——

By the time the Dyson brothers arrived at about 7:00 p.m. at the home of Raymond's father-in-law, Peter Grassfield, the family was just finishing dinner.

Talk turned to the confrontation at the Battle House.

"We were in Mobile about that man, Butler," Raymond said, adding that he had given him a good whipping.

Raymond was satisfied with the beat-down he felt Butler so manifestly deserved, but he had begun to worry about the consequences. Butler was an adulterer, Raymond reasoned, a man of such low character that he surely would "squawk" to the police about the fisticuffs.

"Do you think he will tell about it?" Grassfield asked.

"I don't know. But I am afraid he will," Raymond replied.

Raymond had a plan.

"I want you to do an errand for me," he told his father-in-law, asking Grassfield to see a lawyer in the morning about getting Butler "pinched" for "white slavery." That was a reference to the White Slave Trade Act, commonly referred to as the Mann Act after the 1910 law's author, Representative James Robert Mann.

The statute made it illegal to "transport any woman or girl" across state lines "for any immoral purpose." The Supreme Court ruled in 1913 that Congress had intended this to include "debauchery," not just prostitution. Although rarely enforced today, it remains on the books and was frequently invoked in the first half of the twentieth century. The heavyweight boxing champion, Jack Johnson, was among those convicted under the act for his involvement with a prostitute.

Grassfield agreed to help Raymond but insisted that they go together to see the lawyer and that they had better not wait until the morning. So Raymond showered and put on a white linen suit. Then Grassfield and both of the Dysons set off for Mobile between 8:30 and 9:00 p.m., arriving at about 9:45 p.m.

The car was heading for the home of Robert Gordon, the Mobile County attorney, who lived in the western part of town. The Dysons and Grassfield had trouble finding it but finally pulled up in front of 1325 Dauphin Street at about ten o'clock. Gordon, however, was at the movies. A newsboy walked by shouting "extra" with a report about a sensational slaying at the Battle House.

It was the first time Raymond or his brother realized that they actually had killed Butler.

"I was panic-stricken," Sam would later testify. "We were both panic-stricken and decided the best thing to do was go home and talk to Dad about it."

They never made it home, though. On their way across the causeway connecting Mobile to the eastern shore of Mobile Bay, the Dysons saw a black vehicle with big, red lights that they thought might be a police car. Paranoia began to take hold, and the Dysons asked Grassfield to let them out of the car on the Malbis Road a few miles from the last toll at the base of the bridge. Raymond and Sam hid in the bushes and asked Grassfield to retrieve some clothes from their father's home.

The Dysons' other brother, George, eventually arrived with a car, a change of clothes and some money. Raymond and Sam scrambled out of the bushes and drove off in the greenish Ford DeLuxe Roadster, heading east toward Florida. They arrived in Chattahoochee near the Georgia line. They did not even sleep the first night. Lying in the car, Raymond prayed for guidance.

"Well, I will go back," he told himself.

So the pair turned back and stopped in DeFuniak Springs, a railroad town dating to the nineteenth century. Sam began to worry they'd face rough treatment if the police captured them before they could voluntarily surrender.

"Well, now, if they catch us they will claim we are running away, and they will make it harder for us," he said. "We have got to go there on our free will."

The Dyson boys figured the police would be watching the bridge over Pensacola Bay. They considered taking the road north of Milton but remembered that it did not have any gas stations. So they turned the car around again and headed east. They got to Tallahassee between midnight and 1:00 a.m.

They did not want to wait until the morning, when lawyers' offices would open, so they pushed on to Jacksonville, Florida, on the other side of the state. Exhausted, the Dysons pulled into the first storage garage they saw and parked the car at about 5:30 a.m. They asked an officer where the police station was and then hailed a cab.

Raymond noted the irony of the address to his brother—Liberty Street.

By six o'clock, Raymond and Samuel Dyson had surrendered, telling police there that they had intended "to settle an affair of honor."

———•———

The elegant Battle House Hotel had seen its fair share of history since its first incarnation opened in 1852, constructed on the foundation of the Waverly Hotel, which had burned in 1850. But it likely had experienced nothing as gruesome as the scene that greeted city Detective Mackey White on the evening of August 22, 1932.

The hotel took its name from its proprietors—cotton merchants James, John and Samuel Battle—and persevered through fires and depressions; the owners rebuilt it several times.

It was on this spot that General Andrew Jackson made his headquarters during the War of 1812. It was here that Stephen A. Douglas waited for the presidential election returns on the night he lost to Abraham Lincoln in 1860.

In 1913, five years after the hotel reopened following a devastating 1905 fire, President Woodrow Wilson ate squab (young pigeon) under glass and fruit compote during a breakfast in his honor by the chamber of commerce.

Prominent guests through the years included Confederate president Jefferson Davis, Civil War admiral Raphael Semmes and Confederate generals Braxton Bragg, P.G.T. Beauregard and Richard Taylor.

In the 1930s, the Battle House was the most recognizable hotel in the city, still decades away from its decline and closure and further still from its ultimate rebirth as part of a $200 million investment that resulted in the construction of Alabama's largest skyscraper in 2007.

In Room 552 that evening, mortician James J. Duffy noted the position of the body, paying particular attention to the considerable amount of blood about the head and the black left eye. He removed the bloodstained handkerchief from Butler's mouth.

The investigation quickly turned toward the men who had rented Room 552.

Police did not yet know it, but the Dyson brothers had spent the morning at the Mobile Steel Company pricing materials in preparation for a bid they planned to submit on a project for their contracting company. They ordered lunch at the Metropolitan restaurant on Royal Street, although Raymond could not eat his food. After paying for the meal, they headed for the hotel.

Calhoun, the room clerk, showed investigators the hotel registry. The Dysons had signed their names as S.P. Johnson and R.B. Johnson of Dayton, Ohio. They asked for a room in the remote, northeast corner of the hotel and paid one night's rent in advance.

The porter, Clifton Burnett, escorted them to the chambers while carrying their small, black bag. It contained two shirts, pajamas, underwear, pants and masonry and carpentry statements, although the Dysons had no intention of spending the night. The plan was to drive to the state capital the next day in preparation for the Maxwell Field bid.

The coroner, H.S.J. Walker, examined the body and determined that the cause of death most likely was intracranial bleeding.

Samuel and Raymond Dyson were right to feel paranoid as they sped out of Alabama. It did not take detectives long to trace the phone call the hotel had received to Marmaduke Dyson's home. Police and Mobile County's formidable solicitor, Bart B. Chamberlain, were on his doorstep that night, and before it was over, Marmaduke Dyson was under arrest.

It caused a sensation in Dyson's hometown. He was no ordinary citizen. A founder of the city's famed Single Tax Colony, based on the philosophy of economist Henry George, he also served as the president of the Bank of Fairhope and counted the local newspaper's editors among his friends.

That paper, the *Fairhope Courier*, left no doubt about its sympathies:

The saddest duty which has confronted the editor of this paper is to chronicle a sensational crime involving two of the brightest and most hopeful young

Raymond and Samuel Dyson led Henry M. Butler into Room 552 of the Battle House Hotel, a room very much like this one. *Doy Leale McCall Rare Book and Manuscript Library.*

men, grown to manhood in this community, and two of our most esteemed families; one [sic] *residents here for over a quarter century, linked to the writer and his family by years of the warmest personal friendship and devotion to common and unselfish ideals.*

Butler, too, had come from a prominent family. His father ran a real estate business, and the younger Butler in 1929 was a knight in the Mardi Gras court of King Felix. In December 1930, he married Blossom Sheppard, who also had been a maid—along with the daughter of the judge who would preside over Raymond Dyson's trial—in the Mardi Gras court of Queen Frances Whiting.

The American criminal justice system moved much faster in those days, and by October, prosecutors and defense lawyers were ready for the first trial. Quickly, it became clear that the state versus Raymond Dyson would be a clash of legal titans—Chamberlain for the prosecution, matching wits with defense attorneys Benjamin Franklin McMillan Jr. and Sam Johnston, grandfather of a future Mobile County judge.

Chamberlain and Johnston had squared off against each other months earlier in the trial of Willie Mae Clausen, a thirty-five-year-old woman accused of shooting prominent Mobile lawyer Foster K. Hale Jr. at his law office on June 16, 1931. That trial ended in February 1932 with a conviction on the lesser charge of manslaughter. The judge, Claude A. Grayson, was the same jurist who presided over the Dyson trial.

Chamberlain called the Butler slaying during his opening statement a "cold-blooded and dastardly murder." As the testimony unfolded, it became apparent that the facts would not be in much dispute: The brothers did go to the Battle House with the intention of luring Butler to a confrontation. A fight did follow, and the Dysons did speed away. About the only point contested was intent—the defense insisted Raymond Dyson did not mean to kill his adversary.

The defense lawyers heaped a heavy dose of blame on the victim. Butler, McMillan told jurors, used "art and wiles to seduce" Dorothy Dyson.

In addition to the big guns at the defense table, the defendant had no shortage of leading citizens testifying on his behalf as character witnesses. They included U.S. district attorney Alex C. Birch, Fairhope mayor M.F. Northrup, *Fairhope Courier* editor E.B. Gaston, Baldwin County Probate Court judge G.W. Humphries and Dyson's architecture professor at Auburn University.

The trial consumed Mobile. Some people sat in the darkened courtroom for up to an hour each morning before the beginning of proceedings to ensure they got a seat. Dorothy Dyson, dressed in a black, tailored suit and coat, black shoes, gray stockings and a thin black veil covering her face on the day of jury selection, was a focal point of spectators' attention throughout the trial.

As the *Mobile Register* put it, spectators viewed her with a mixture of "curiosity, scorn and admiration."

The victim's sister sat a few feet from Dorothy, rarely taking her eyes off her. At the start of the trial, Dorothy's "face radiated its cheerfulness," a newsman wrote, while the victim's sister's face maintained sadness. Butler's father sat with his back to the Dysons, seldom speaking a word.

The *Mobile Register* waxed poetic: "The hearing, despite the sordidness of the revelation, seemed to bring a nearer presence that that great human thing which is called law, in that great Divine thing which is called justice."

A native of Tipton, Iowa, Dorothy Grassfield had moved to Fairhope with her parents in May 1925 when she was eighteen years old. She married Raymond Dyson in May of the following year and gave birth on July 28, 1927, to their first child, Barbara. In September 1929, Raymond left for Auburn to finish his architecture degree.

With her husband away, Dorothy met the handsome, young Henry Butler in January 1930 at the home of a friend. They went to a dance one night, and on another evening, she watched him play basketball. About a month later, she ran into him on a street in Mobile.

Butler saw her again while she was driving her father's car, and he asked if he could see her. "Yes," she said, inviting him to return that evening.

He did come that night, and Dorothy and her young daughter went for a drive. Another day, Butler asked Dorothy to lunch, but she was on her way to Montgomery to visit her husband, on a break from his studies. So Butler gave her a ride to the train station.

When Dorothy returned, she had dinner with Butler at the home of a friend, and then they went to the movies. Afterward, Butler and Dorothy went for a drive again.

When Dorothy was in a Fairhope tearoom, Butler arrived with a crowd of friends. Later, they went to the home of Virginia Steele, who told Dorothy she had never been to New Orleans. Steele asked her friend if she wanted to go with her.

Dorothy agreed, and when she met Steele in Bienville Square on March 22, 1930, Butler drove up with another man, Louis Sauer. She was surprised when conversation in the car turned to the sleeping arrangements as the vehicle passed through the New Orleans suburb of Slidell.

It was clear that each of the women was to spend the night with her date. Dorothy protested, but Steele teased her for being a "wet blanket." Butler and Sauer registered at the Roosevelt Hotel with their "wives."

At the time, Dorothy already was pregnant with her second child.

The foursome returned on March 24. Dorothy told Butler she could not see him again. He persisted, and she did see him a few more times before breaking off the affair for good.

Dorothy's dalliances had begun to attract whispered notice in small-town Fairhope, however, and those rumors eventually reached the ears of her husband.

Raymond rushed home from Auburn in June 1930 after his pregnant wife had been admitted to Providence Hospital for a possible miscarriage. His roommate at Auburn, William McIntosh Jr., told him that he had been a dinner guest at Dorothy's house three months earlier. He said he took Dorothy's friend, Virginia, home late that evening. While walking past the Dyson house later that night, he saw Butler dropping Dorothy off at about midnight.

Confronted by her husband, Dorothy confessed to having "dates" but nothing more, and Raymond believed her. The miscarriage scare over, Dorothy ended up giving birth to a baby boy, Bromley, on July 30, 1930.

The rumors of an affair seemed forgotten. But a careless phrase thrust them to the surface in April 1932. The couple had just spent a lovely Sunday at the Gulf of Mexico. They were lying in the bedroom. Raymond felt especially close to his wife and told her, "Honey, I have never loved any other woman but you."

Raymond was taken aback when he saw tears roll down Dorothy's cheek. She told her husband that she was not the same woman she was when he married her but refused to give more details. She tried to retract the statement. "I don't mean that," she said. "I have never loved anyone else."

But the seeds of doubt had been sewn. Raymond had trouble eating or sleeping over the next several weeks. He would get up to turn on the radio, only to shut it off moments later. About May 20, 1932, Raymond sat on the couch with his wife, clasped her hand and demanded a full explanation.

"Honey, tell me everything so I can get the thing out of my mind and through with," he said.

Dorothy confessed that she had gone with H.M. Butler to Bailey's Creek near Fairhope.

"That was a great shock to me, because I had never had but one love," Raymond later recalled from the witness stand.

Raymond had dismissed the rumors in the past, even lashing out at a comment by his own father. Now that he had a confession from his wife's mouth, he was distraught.

"It seems what they've been saying about Dorothy is true," he told Sam.

The couple attempted reconciliation during a second honeymoon in California for their sixth wedding anniversary in May 1932. They met friends of Dorothy from Iowa and considered starting a new life there. But after three weeks, Raymond could not find contracting work. He was depressed throughout the trip and accused his wife of not being fit to be a mother. He threatened to take the children away.

In July, Raymond was looking through one of his architecture textbooks and found a program for the Little Theatre in New Orleans. Remembering Dorothy had told him that she was going to visit the city with a friend while he was at Auburn, he asked Dorothy what really happened during that trip. She admitted she had spent the night with Butler.

A wave of rage rolled over him.

Dorothy broke down on the witness stand when she described the scene. "He seemed to lose control of his mind," she told the jury. "He went insane, you might say."

Raymond stormed out of the house and returned drunk at three o'clock in the morning. He demanded to know if Dorothy was "Butler's woman." She answered yes but begged for forgiveness. He accused her of being unfit to be a mother.

The next morning, Dorothy asked her husband if he had meant what he said. When he responded in the affirmative, she walked despondent into the bathroom and swallowed a bichloride of mercury tablet, a common antiseptic that had become a popular suicide tool. She was starting to take another when Raymond knocked it from her hand. He sent his five-year-old daughter to fetch some flour and then mixed it with water and mustard to make an antidote. He slapped his wife across the face to force her to swallow the solution.

Dorothy vomited blue liquid all over the floor.

She lingered for five days before finally recovering. But there was no recovering from the chasm that now was dividing the couple.

Later in July, Dorothy's friend Francis McConnell told Raymond that his wife was not sure who Bromley's father was.

Raymond asked his wife one day if she had been to see Butler. She said no. He asked her if she preferred Butler. She told Raymond that he could never be the man Butler was. She meant it as a compliment, that Raymond never would compromise his morals and seduce a married woman. But Raymond misinterpreted the comment as a put-down, and it sent him into a fury. Dorothy slapped him during the ensuing argument; he threw a chair into the kitchen and injured his wrist against the door. He slammed his fist through a window pane and bled all over the house.

With blood spurting from Raymond's wound, Dorothy tried to bandage it. But he yanked it away. "To hell with it!" he screamed. "Let it bleed."

Another day, Raymond punched his own jaw so hard that he almost dislocated it.

"It seemed sometimes like I was in a dungeon," Raymond later recalled in court. "I would feel these [thoughts] coming on me, and I felt as if like there were four walls closing down on me. I just had to hit something. One time I hit my jaw several times. It was almost dislocated. It was real sore."

The couple began to discuss separation. Dorothy told her husband that he could have Barbara but that Bromley was hers. She meant that Bromley favored her side of the family while Barbara was more like a Dyson. But the already fragile Dyson interpreted the comment as a commentary on the boy's paternity.

Raymond got a trunk, packed it with Dorothy's clothes and took it to her father's house. A week later, Dorothy was gone, on her way to California. It was mid-August 1932, about a week and a half before the bloodshed at the Battle House. Dorothy ended up spending twenty days alone in the Golden State.

On August 16, Raymond received a letter from his wife:

> *Dear Raymond, if I only knew what was going on in your mind I would know better how to write…I hope you will take good care of my babies. Tell me what you have done about getting somebody to mother them? I am sorry I have made such a mess or our lives.*

The same day, he wrote to her:

> *Dear Donie: Oh, I have missed you. I hope you are getting some good clean air in your lungs out there in the Pacific. Donie, I still love you. We are all God's creatures and have to take things as they are and try to see the beauty and art in life.*

Days before the killing, though, Raymond discovered an old letter Butler had sent to a friend discussing his desire to see Dorothy. It set off Raymond anew.

The stage was set for the "affair of honor."

——•——

During closing arguments of the closely watched trial, the defense tried to convince the jury that Henry Butler cast his own fate by seducing a married woman. Attorney Sam Johnston depicted Dorothy Dyson as a victim who had been "violated" by Butler.

"It is sad when the young men of our country feel that they have a right to go out and seduce any young woman they see fit," he said.

Solicitor Bart Chamberlain depicted the slaying as cold-blooded and premeditated.

"The state of Alabama does not apologize for terming this a cowardly, gang killing," he said.

When it came time for the jury to render a verdict, the decision was not difficult. The jurors deliberated for just twenty-three minutes, returning to pronounce the thirty-year-old defendant "not guilty."

The announcement of the verdict elicited cheers from the spectators. Raymond sat at the defense table as if in a daze. Behind him, Dorothy's face was covered in tears. She reached forward and touched her husband's shoulder. He clasped her hand to his breast.

Defense attorney Benjamin McMillan Jr. grabbed his client's hand. The family gathered, and Dorothy fainted; she had to be carried to an adjacent room.

Raymond praised the jury as he left the courthouse.

"I want to thank them all for what they have done for Dorothy," he said. "I am sorry this thing ever happened. I would not have had it happen for the world."

The *Mobile Register* blared the result across the front page the next morning.

"Two year old Bromley Dyson's dad came home to him last night for a jury in criminal court had acquitted him of the slaying of the man who refused to assure him that Bromley was a Dyson," the story began.

Raymond Dyson now was a free man, who would go on to a long and lucrative career as a building contractor. The verdict came on the same day Willie Mae Clausen—the defendant in the previous Chamberlain-versus-Johnston legal battle—got out of jail.

Despite the defeat, prosecutors elected to move forward with the case against Sam Dyson. But it did not go any better for Solicitor Chamberlain than the first trial had.

On February 2, 1933, a jury took even less time than his brother's jurors had—fewer than five minutes—to decide that the defendant was not guilty.

BIBLIOGRAPHY

CHAPTER 1

Burton, C.M. *In the Footsteps of Cadillac*. Detroit, MI: Wolverine Printing Company, 1899.

———. *A Sketch of the Life of Antoine de la Mothe Cadillac, Founder of Detroit*. Detroit, MI: Wilton-Smith, 1895.

Craighead, Erwin. *Mobile: Fact and Tradition*. Mobile, AL: Powers Printing Company, 1930.

Dawson, Joseph, III, ed. *The Louisiana Governors: From Iberville to Edwards*. Baton Rouge: Louisiana State University Press, 1990.

Delaney, Caldwell, and Clark S. Whistler. *Remember Mobile*. Mobile, AL: Haunted Book Shop, 1980.

Giraud, Marcel. *A History of French Louisiana: The Reign of Louis XIV, 1698–1715*. Baton Rouge: Louisiana State University, 1974.

Higginbotham, Jay. *Old Mobile: Fort Louis de la Louisiane, 1702–1711*. Tuscaloosa: University of Alabama Press, 1991.

Laut, Agnes C. *Cadillac, Knight Errant of the Wilderness, Founder of Detroit, Governor of Louisiana from the Great Lakes to the Gulf*. Indianapolis, IN: Bobbs-Merrill Company, 1931.

Reeves, Miriam. *The Governors of Louisiana*. Gretna, LA: Pelican Publishing Company, 1972.

Wilds, John, Charles L. Dufour and Walter G. Cowan. *Louisiana Yesterday and Today: A Historical Guide to the State*. Baton Rouge: Louisiana State University Press, 1996.

Zoltvany, Yves F. "LAUMET, de Lamothe Cadillac, ANTOINE." *Dictionary of Canadian Biography*. Vol. 2. University of Toronto/Université Laval, 2003– . http://www.biographi.ca/en/bio/laumet_antoine_2E.html.

CHAPTER 2

Coley, C.J. "Creek Treaties, 1790–1832." *Alabama Review*, 1958.

Griffith, Benjamin, Jr. *McIntosh and Weatherford: Creek Indian Leaders*. Tuscaloosa: University of Alabama Press, 1988.

Halbert, Henry S., and T.H. Ball. *The Creek War of 1813 and 1814*. Tuscaloosa: University of Alabama Press, 1895.

Hall, Arthur H. "The Red Stick War." *Chronicles of Oklahoma* 12, no. 3 (September 1934).

Mobile Daily Register. "An Old Man Tells His Tale Of Long Ago." September 28, 1884.

Parker, Prescott Alphonso. *Story of the Tensaw: Blakely, Spanish Fort, Jackson Oaks, Fort Mims*. Montrose, AL: P.A. Parker, 1922.

Pickett, Albert James. *History of Alabama and Incidentally of Georgia and Mississippi from the Earliest Period*. Charleston, SC: Walker and James, 1851.

Thompson, Lynn Hastie. *William Weatherford: His Country and His People*. Bay Minette, AL: Lavender Publishing Company, 1991.

Waselkov, Gregory A. *A Conquering Spirit: Fort Mims and the Redstick War of 1813–1814*. Tuscaloosa: University of Alabama Press, 2006.

CHAPTER 3

Albany Evening Journal. "Wrong Man Hung [*sic*]." August 23, 1847.

Boyington, Charles. *A Statement of the Trial of Charles R.S. Boyington, Who Was Indicted and Executed for the Murder of Nathaniel Frost*. Mobile, AL: Mobile Mercantile Advertiser. 1835.

Craighead, Erwin. *From Mobile's Past: Sketches of Memorable People and Events*. Mobile, AL: Powers Printing Company, 1925.

Delchamps, J.J. Letter to the editor. *Mobile Register.* August 9, 1870.

Diard, François Ludgére. *The Tree: Being the Strange Case of Charles R.S. Boyington*. Mobile, AL: Gill Printing Company, 1949.

Garrett, Ephraim S. "Remember Boyington! Mobile's Amazing Mystery." *True Detective Mysteries*, April 1934.

Hamilton, William T. *The Last Hours of Charles R.S. Boyington: Who Was Executed at Mobile, Alabama, for the Murder of Nathaniel Frost. Perpetrated May 10, 1834*. Mobile, AL: Commercial Register Office, 1835.

Johnson, Alvin. "Tree Growing Through Grave 'Proving' Innocence of Charles Boyington." Unknown newspaper and date, on file at in the Charles Boyington file at the Mobile Public Library.

"Man Hanged Long Ago in Mobile." August 30, 1936. Unknown newspaper, on file at the Mobile History Museum.

Mobile County Circuit Court minute book, November 3, 1834.

Mobile Daily Commercial Register and Patriot. "Arrest of Boyington." May 15, 1834.

———. "Commitment of Boyington." May 17, 1834.

———. "Execution." February 21, 1835.

———. "Murder." May 12, 1834.

———. "Murder!!! 500 Dollars Reward!" May 13, 1834.

————. "Obituary. The Late Nathaniel Frost." May 14, 1834.

————. "Verdict." November 22, 1834

Mobile Daily Register. "Reminiscences of Mobile." July 6, 1879.

Mobile Mercantile Advertiser. "Shocking Murder." May 12, 1834.

Poore, Ralph. "Boyington Oak a Local Legend." *Mobile Press*, May 1, 1989.

Porter, Benjamin F. "Reminiscences of Benjamin F. Porter." Unpublished memoir on file at Mobile History Museum, n.d.

————. *Reports of Cases at Law and in Equity Argued and Adjudged in the Supreme Court of Alabama.* Vol. 2. Tuscaloosa, AL: Marmaduke J. Slade, 1836.

Pruitt, Paul M., Jr., and Robert Bond Higgins. "Crime and Punishment in Antebellum Mobile: The Long Story of Charles R.S. Boyington." *Gulf Coast Historical Review* 11, no. 2 (Spring 1996).

Chapter 4

Alabama Planter. Untitled article. April 1, 1849.

Beverly, Frances. *Copeland's Hide Out.* Historical collection of the Works Progress Administration.

Dana, David. *The Fireman: The Fire Departments of the United States, with a Full Account of All Large Fires, Statistics of Losses on Expenses, Theatres Destroyed by Fire and Accidents, Anecdotes and Incidents.* Boston: French and Company, 1858.

Mobile Daily Register. "City Court." February 25, 1859.

————. "City Court." March 4, 1858.

————. "The State vs. Pitts." March 5, 1859.

Penick, James. "James Copeland and Sheriff Pitts: A Gulf Coast Legend." *Gulf Coast Historical Review* 2, no. 2 (Spring 1987).

Pitts, J.R.S. *Life and Confession of the Noted Outlaw James Copeland.* 1909. Reprint, Hattiesburg: University Press of Mississippi, 1980.

Russell, Carrie. "Outlaw Days." Historical Research Project No. 2983. Unpublished project on file at the Mobile History Museum, 1936.

Sledge, John. *The Pillared City: Greek Revival Mobile.* Athens: University of Georgia Press, 2009.

————. "Port City Street Cred." *Mobile Bay Monthly*, February 2012.

Stovall, William H. *Strange Stories Behind Pension Claims.* Philadelphia: Dorrance & Company Inc., 1935.

Chapter 5

Chernin, Eli. "Josiah Clark Nott, Insects and Yellow Fever." *Bulletin of the New York Academy of Medicine*, November 1983.

Craighead, Erwin. *Mobile Fact and Tradition: Noteworthy People and Events.* Mobile, AL: Powers Printing Company, 1930.

De Gobineau, A., and Nott, J.C. *The Moral and Intellectual Diversity of Races.* Philadelphia: J.B. Lippincott & Co., 1856.

East, Cammie. "Mobile's Dr. Nott Is Not Forgotten." *Mobile Register*, May 30, 1976.

Flower, Frank A. *History of the Republican Party: Embracing Its Origin, Growth and Mission.* Springfield, IL: Union Publishing Company, 1884.

Horseman, Reginald. *Josiah Nott of Mobile: Southerner, Physician and Racial Theorist.* Baton Rouge: Louisiana State University Press, 1987.

The Nationalist. "The School at Medical College." February 15, 1866.

Nott, Josiah. "Life Insurance at the South." *Commercial Review of the South and West 3,* no. 5 (May 1847).

————. *Two Lectures on the Connection Between the Biblical and Physical History of Man.* New York: Bartlett and Welford, 1849.

Wade, Richard C. *Slavery in the Cities: The South, 1820–1860.* New York: Oxford University Press, 1964.

CHAPTER 6

Alabama Department of History and Archives. "Alabama Civil War Service Database." http://archives.state.al.us/civilwar/search.cfm.

Cain, Joe. "Myths and Mardi Gras in Mobile—The Mother of Mystics." Unknown newspaper, on file at the Mobile History Museum, n.d.

Craighead, Erwin. *Mobile Fact and Tradition.* Mobile, AL: Powers Printing Company, 1930.

Daugherty, Frank. "Keep at It, Judy, at It." *Azalea City News & Review.* February 26, 1981.

Dean, Wayne. "Symbols of the Old South in Mobile's Mardi Gras." *Mobile Bay Monthly*, February 1989.

Higginbotham, Jay. *Old Mobile: Fort Louis de la Louisiane, 1702–1711.* Tuscaloosa: University of Alabama Press, 1991.

Hoffman, Roy. "Raising Cains." *Mobile Register*, February 6, 2005.

Joynt, Steve. "Changing His Story." *Mobile Mask*, 2015.

Kent, Mark. "Joe Cain Is the Immortal Spirit of Mardi Gras." *Mobile Register*, February 12, 1994.

Laborde, Errol "The Men Who Made Mardi Gras." *New Orleans Magazine*, February 2002.

McDonnell, Harry. "Joe Cain to Rest Again in City He Made Happier." *Mobile Press Register.* December 25, 1966.

Mobile County News. "Joe Cain at Home." January 26, 1967.

Mobile Daily Register. "Mardi-Gras, First Celebration by the O.O.M." February 26, 1868.

————. "The No. 8 Horses." February 26, 1868.

Mobile Register. "Death of Joseph S. Cain." April 19, 1904.

Potts, Charlie. "Slacabamarinico Lives." *Azalea City News & Review.* February 26, 1981.

Rayford, Julian. "Centennial for Bayou's Joe Cain." *Mobile County News*, February 10, 1966.

————. *Chasin' the Devil Round a Stump.* Mobile, AL: American Print Company, 1962.

Roberts, L. Craig. *Mardi Gras in Mobile.* Charleston, SC: The History Press, 2015.

Chapter 7

Alabama Lawyers Association. "Judge Roderick B. Thomas, Alabama's First Black Judge." http://www.ala-lawyers.org/judge-roderick-b-thomas.

Amos, Harriet E. "Trials of a Unionist: Gustavus Horton, Military Mayor of Mobile During Reconstruction." *Gulf Coast Historical Review* 4, no. 2 (Spring 1989).

Brent, Joseph E. "No Compromise: The End of Presidential Reconstruction in Mobile, Alabama, January–May 1867." *Gulf Coast Historical Review* 7, no. 1 (Fall 1991).

Burnett, Lonnie A. *The Pen Makes a Good Sword: John Forsyth of the* Mobile Register. Tuscaloosa: University of Alabama Press, 2006.

Fitzgerald, Michael. *Urban Emancipation: Popular Politics in Reconstruction Mobile, 1860–1890.* Baton Rouge: Louisiana State University Press, 2002.

Mobile Advertiser "The Civil Rights Bill in Mobile—Examination of the Mayor." August 13, 1867

Mobile Daily Register. "Judge Kelley And Col. Mann." May 20, 1888.

Mobile Daily Times. "The Kelley Disturbance." 1867.

Mobile Sunday Times (reprinted from the *Omaha Herald*). "The Alabamians Are Coming." 1868.

Nationalist. "The Attitude of the North Toward the South." February 15, 1866.

———. "The Jury Question." November 7, 1867.

———. "Northern Man in the South." February 15, 1866.

New York Times. "The Bread Riot in Mobile; Two Outbreaks in One Day. Arrivals in the City." May 28, 1867. Reprinted from the September 21 *New Orleans Era*.

———. "The Case of Mayor Horton, of Mobile." December 27, 1867.

———. "The Civil Rights Case in Mobile." April 8, 1867.

———. "THE FREEDMEN: Further Details from Major-Gen. Howard's Reports Operations and Results in the Different States." December 25, 1865.

———. "The Mayor of Mobile Arrested for Violation of the Civil Rights Bill." August 10, 1867.

———. "Preservation of the Public Peach in the Third Military District—Order from Gen. Pope." June 4, 1867.

———. "The Recent Changes in Municipal Officers—Protest of the Ex-Mayor—Gen. Swayne's Report Upon the Riot—Result of the Coroner's Inquest." May 28, 1867.

———. "The Riot at Mobile." May 16, 1867.

———. "Terrible Calamity at Mobile." May 30, 1865.

Schurz, Carl. *Report on the Condition of the South.* Report to the Thirty-ninth Congress, 1865.

Chapter 8

American Banner. "A Colored Boy in Trouble." October 19, 1901.

———. "Notes and Personals." October 19, 1901.

———. "Our Trip to Daphne." October 19, 1901.

BIBLIOGRAPHY

Crosby, Samuel. *The Sleeping Juror & Other Baldwin County Courtroom Tales & History.* Montgomery, AL: Law Foundation, 2002.

Crowder, Joan White. *Tell It to an Old Hollow Log: Growing UP in Daphne, Alabama.* Bay Minette, AL: Lavender Publishing, 2000.

Fairhope Courier. "Fairhope Is Shocked by Terrible Tragedy." August 25, 1932.

Gould, Elizabeth Barrett. *From Fort to Port: An Architectural History of Mobile, Alabama, 1711–1918.* Tuscaloosa: University of Alabama Press, 1988.

Hellmann, Paul T. *Historical Gazetteer of the United States.* New York: Routledge, 2004.

Kirby, Brendan. "Probate Judge's Participation in Courthouse 'Theft' Disputed." *Mobile Register,* July 27, 2001.

Mobile County website. "Mobile Government Plaza History of Mobile County Courthouses." http://www.mobilecountyal.gov/government/govt_plaza_courthouse.html.

Mobile News Item. "Lively Times at Daphne." October 13, 1901.

Mobile Press-Register. "Bay Minette 'Swiped' Seat of Baldwin County in 1901." September 20, 1946.

Nuzum, Kay. *A History of Baldwin County.* Bay Minette, AL: Baldwin Times, 1971.

Owen, Thomas McAdory. *History of Alabama and Dictionary of Alabama Biography.* Chicago: S.J. Clarke Publishing Company, 1921.

Partin, Charles. "The 1901 Removal of Baldwin County Seat Revisited." *Historical and Genealogical Quarterly* 3, nos. 1–4 (1991–92).

Scott, Florence Dolive Scott. *Daphne: A History of Its People as Some Saw It and Others Remember It.* Mobile, AL: Jordan Printing Company, Inc., 1965.

Southern Reporter 33, containing all the decisions of the Supreme Courts of Alabama, Louisiana, Florida, Mississippi. December 20, 1902–April 25, 1903. *Hand et al v. Stapleton et al.*

Southern Reporter 37, containing all the decisions of the Supreme Courts of Alabama, Louisiana, Florida, Mississippi. July 30, 1904–March 25, 1905. *Hand et al v. Stapleton et al.*

Southern Reporter 39, containing all the decisions of the Supreme Courts of Alabama, Louisiana, Florida, Mississippi. September 2, 1905–March 10, 1906. *Hand et al v. Stapleton et al.*

CHAPTER 9

Alsobrook, David E. *Alabama's Port City: Mobile During the Progressive Era, 1896–1917.* PhD diss., Auburn University, 1983.

Chamberlain, Bart B., to Governor Thomas Kilby, June 16, 1919. On file at the Mobile History Museum.

Drago, John, to Governor B.B. Comer, April 13, 1908, and November 7, 1908. On file at the Mobile History Museum.

Flynt, Wayne. *Alabama in the Twentieth Century.* Tuscaloosa: University of Alabama Press, 2004.

Hamburger, Max, to J.H. Nunnelee, November 20, 1908. Comer Papers. On file at the Mobile History Museum.

BIBLIOGRAPHY

Hamilton, Peter J., to Governor B.B. Comer, January 21, 1907. On file at the Mobile History Museum.

Hamilton, Virginia Van der Veer. *Hugo Black: The Alabama Years.* Baton Rouge: Louisiana State University Press, 1972.

Higginbotham, Jay. *Mobile! City by the Bay.* Mobile, AL: Azalea City Printers, 1968.

Hodges, Sam. "Teflon Tycoon." *Mobile Register*, December 19, 2001.

Holcombe, William H., to Governor Thomas Kilby, July 18, 1919. On file at the Mobile History Museum.

Inge, Mrs. H.T., to Governor B.B. Comer, January 27, 1907. On file at the Mobile History Museum.

Lee, Lawrence H. *Report of Cases Argued and Determined in the Supreme Court of Alabama During the November Term, 1908–1909.* Montgomery, AL: Brown Printing Company, 1910.

Lyons, A.S., to Governor B.B. Comer, September 21, 1907. On file at the Mobile History Museum.

Mitchell, H.H., to Governor B.B. Comer, May 10, 1908. On file at the Mobile History Museum.

Mobile Daily Herald. "Local Self-Government." March 1908.

Mobile Register. "Deputy Tells of Raids on Shinny Makers by Force." December 5, 1920.

———. "McLaurin, Deputy Slayer, Faces Trial Before Great Judge." May 16, 1921.

———. "McLaurin Guarded as Warrant Served." March 10, 1921.

———. "Mobile Waits as Rumors of Sensation Grow." November 15, 1923.

———. "U.S. Men Swoop Down on Liquor Traffic Here." November 12, 1923.

———. "U.S. Men Unfold Evidence in Liquor Probe." April 14, 1924.

———. "Young M'Laurin Gives Statement in Shooting Case." March 5, 1921.

New York Times. "Live Wire, Flares and Guns Guard Mobile Liquor Cache." November 19, 1923.

Sellers, James Benson. *The Prohibition Movement in Alabama, 1702–1943.* Chapel Hill: University of North Carolina Press, 1943.

Thompson, William W., to Governor B.B. Comer, January 21, 1907. On file at the Mobile History Museum.

Webb, Samuel L. "The Great Mobile Whiskey War." *Alabama Heritage*, Spring 2005.

CHAPTER 10

Craighead, Erwin. *Mobile Fact and Tradition, Noteworthy People and Events.* Mobile, AL: Powers Printing Company, 1930.

Fairhope Courier. "Fairhope Is Shocked By Terrible Tragedy." August 25, 1932.

Gormley, Bill. "Dyson Acquitted in Slaying." *Mobile Times*, November 14, 1932.

———. "Dyson Case to Reach Jury Late in Day." *Mobile Times*, November 14, 1932.

———. "Dyson Testifies for Brother." *Mobile Times*, November 11, 1932.

———. "Testimony Is Ended in Dyson Murder Trial." *Mobile Sunday Times*, November 13, 1932.

Green, Matt. Interview with the author. January 2015.

BIBLIOGRAPHY

Historic Hotels of America. "Battle House Renaissance Mobile Hotel & Spa." http://www.historichotels.org/hotels-resorts/battle-house-renaissance-mobile-hotel-and-spa/history.php.

Jumper, Kathy "RSA Project Has Foot in Two Centuries." *Mobile Register*, April 29, 2007.

MacPhail, Rhodes. "Jury Expected to Get Dyson Case Late Monday." *Mobile Press Register*, November 13, 1932.

————. "Raymond Dyson Is Acquitted of Slaying Butler." *Mobile Register*, November 15, 1932.

————. "Raymond Dyson Takes Stand Today in Defense." *Mobile Register*, November 12 1932.

————. "Spectators Ponder Query on 'Innocence or Guilt' as Dyson Case Continues." *Mobile Register*, November 14, 1932.

————. "State Is Nearing End of Evidence in Trial of Dyson." *Mobile Register*, November 11, 1932.

Mobile Register. "Arraignment of Pair Set for Monday." October 23, 1932.

————. "Dyson Jury to Get Case Late in Day." November 14, 1932.

————. "Dysons File Not Guilty Plea in Case." October 25, 1932.

————. "Jury Named in Dyson Trial." November 10, 1932.

————. "Mobile Real Estate Man Slain in Hotel Room." August 23, 1932.

————. "Sam Dyson Acquitted in Butler Slaying Case." February 3, 1933.

————. "Sam Dyson Opens Defense as State Ends Testimony." February 2, 1933.

————. "Search for Butler Killers Spreads Over Dixie." August 24, 1932.

Mobile Times. "Butler's Father Takes the Stand." November 10, 1932.

————. "Dyson Kisses Wife in Court." October 23, 1932.

————. "Full and Descriptive Story of Dyson Murder Hearing." November 11, 1932.

————. "Samuel Tells How Brother and Butler Had Fight." November 13, 1932.

Politico. "Congress Passes the White Slave Traffic Act, June 25, 1910." June 25, 2010.

ABOUT THE AUTHOR

*B*rendan Kirby is a senior political reporter for *LifeZette.com*. He worked for the *Mobile Press-Register* and *Al.com* for fifteen years prior to that, covering a variety of beats. He has a great interest in history.

Brendan began his career in 1994 for the *Northwest Current* in Washington, D.C. He worked for four years for the *Herald-Mail* in Hagerstown, Maryland, where his met his wife, Kerry. They live in Daphne, Alabama, with their two children, Mariah and Declan; their dog, Tillie; and cat, Martin.

Brendan grew up in the Philadelphia suburbs and shares that region's fanatical devotion to the Phillies, Eagles, Flyers and 76ers.

Visit us at
www.historypress.net
....

This title is also available as an e-book